Say What! Sayings of the Sage

A collection of short musings on life from a home(personal) and work(professional) perspective

Glenn D. Stevens

Disclaimer:

All images contained in this book are generated using artificial intelligence (AI). They are not based on real individuals, events, or actual places. Any resemblance to real persons, living or dead, or to actual events is purely coincidental. The images are intended for illustrative purposes only and should not be interpreted as reflective of reality.

Readership

Life, what exactly about it that makes it so intriguing and at the same time so challenging. This book encourages the reader to pause, to slow down, and take some time to think before going on to the next thing. It seeks to provide stimulating insights into different aspects of life and living, challenging the reader to look beneath the rocks. It is filled with puns to take the sharp edge of life, allowing us to smell the roses while we still have noses. It takes a witty approach to the gravity of living, whereby the reader can reflect, think, ruminate, and ponder on its message. The book is not an authority on any topic and is meant to be read by those who want to learn from those who have made mistakes and kick themselves for overlooking the obvious. It seeks to enlighten the room with a light spin on getting the best from life without losing their skin in the act of doing so. Relax, pull up a chair, get a cup of tea, and let the sweet aroma of the lyrics marinate your mind and shape your thinking.

Acknowledgment

I am indebted to my Lord and Savior, Jesus Christ, for affording me the opportunities to enjoy living to the fullest and being able to pen these thoughts. I thank my wife, Ann, and my children, Gregg, Jonmarc and Gabrielle, for their input and ingredients in the material provided to whom I dedicate this book. For having to endure the brunt of my philosophy on living, I thank my work colleagues at the Home Depot for bearing with me and allowing me to share my thoughts with them through my weekly blog, meetings, and team-building events.

My desire is for those who read this collection of thoughts to take some time to reflect on life, its true meaning and significance, and in so doing, have a more fulfilling and rewarding life.

Build....
Grow....
Serve......

Bio

Glenn is an IT professional specializing in software quality engineering and enterprise software business systems delivery management. His extensive career covers leadership roles in both the telecommunications and retail industries, with tenures at Cable & Wireless, GTE, Schlumberger, Macy's, and The Home Depot. A servant-leader at heart, Glenn is committed to guiding and helping others to achieve their personal and professional goals and aspirations.

Outside of work, Glenn finds joy in life's simple pleasures. He values the time spent with his family, mentoring others, the excitement of travel, photography, and the joy of writing. Glenn currently resides in Georgia with his wife of over 40 years, nurturing a home filled with love and memories.

Contents

1 Wearing pajamas to work

Attitude, what exactly is it, and why do we even have it?

It is sometimes invisible to us but quite often very evident to others. We are the owners of our attitudes and have the power to influence others around us for better or for worse.

All of us at some time or another, get out of bed on the wrong side, not properly dressed for the day. Yes, we sometimes show up for work in our attitude pajamas.

Even worse yet, we fail to bathe and put on clean clothing (if you get my drift). We expect the world to open the door as we go through the routine of getting ready to leave the house, only to find out the car is locked with the keys misplaced.

The kids have not done their homework; the pipe is now leaking, and the refrigerator needs a water filter. We encounter traffic along the way, and we have to wait for the person to cross the street who has no urgency in the world. So, by the time we reach the office, our attitude attire is really crumpled.

We complain about the little things we take so much for granted that appear to be out of place. We get grumpy and miserable. We forget that we are still wearing our PJs.

How do we get out of our pajamas, you say? See the day as one filled with opportunities for you to make a positive difference. Give a polite greeting to those you meet during your morning routine. How about doing something kind and thoughtful for another person that you would not normally do? Exercising more patience rather than being demanding. Being more friendly and engaging instead of being rough, rude and crude. How about just being grateful, period?

So, instead of ruining the remainder of your day, remember the fact that at least you can get out of bed compared to others who are unable to do so. Think about the fact that there will be some who will not return to their beds at the end of the day. Count it a blessing that you are able to get out of bed, do your stuff, and return to bed. So, there you have it. Leave your pajamas at home before going out for the day; your attitude will thank you for this, not to mention your mental health, emotional and physical well-being.

I used to complain about the fact that I had no shoes until I met a man who had no feet.

(Indian proverb)

2 Who is your guard rail?

Very often, you hear the cry, "Our freedom matters!" We need to have the freedom to do as we please; America is a free country, and our freedom comes first. But with any true freedom comes responsibilities and boundaries. Before you execute an action in the spirit of freedom, do you consider the impact of that action on a partner or team member, the outcome on a future position on others or yourself?

I believe a more responsible form of expressing freedom is one where we have guard rails in place. Guard rails serve to keep us from falling off the edge, keeping us on the safe side. They are there to caution us and sometimes restrain us when our "freedom" wants to get the better of us.

A guard rail can be a colleague, an accountable partner, a team member who you can confide in and will provide honest feedback, or someone who can help to keep you "safe" from the dangers and perils of faulty decisions.

In family settings, this means having a trusted confidante who you can readily go to for advice who is not afraid to tell you where you need to change. In relationship settings, it is having a friend who is candid and can give sound, unbiased advice. Someone you know who will not just tell you the ugly truth you don't want to hear but will also provide you with tips on how to move forward safely.

Who is your guard rail that prevents you from going over the edge, landing in the ditch, or going off at the deep end?

You only know some people are swimming naked when the tide goes out.

(Warren Buffet)

3 Failure plans

“Failing to plan is planning to fail” was echoed by Sir Winston Churchill to his wartime generals during WW II. Yet so many of us launch out into getting our work done without effectively planning how the work is to be done. Planning by itself is not enough to warrant success; however, it is one of the key essentials in contributing to a successful outcome when done right.

Do we know in advance what we want to accomplish? Do we take into consideration the things we will need to have success? Do we consider those things we call risks and weigh them against how they could negatively impact the desired outcome? Have we identified milestone markers we can use to tell us how well we are doing against the planned course of action?

Here then, is a simple outline for effective planning:

1. Identify goals and objectives and the benefits or values you expect to achieve.

2. Identify the resources needed, along with any supporting roles and responsibilities.

3. Determine the steps and actions necessary, in order to achieve the goals.

4. Establish some means to measure progress and track actuals against targets and the frequency of doing so.

5. Identify risks and potential issues and determine what mitigations and contingencies are required.

One of the most profound failures to plan effectively is seen when people get into retirement. More and more people are reaching retirement without the necessary finances to live decently. What if they started planning early enough in their younger life when they had the means to save for their retirement?

Planning is hard work, but when done right, it far outweighs the gratification of just leaving things to luck. Do make sure your plan is sound. Run it by others or get input from others who can help you develop a solid working plan. A bad plan is as good as no plan; a good plan that is poorly executed is as bad as not having a plan. How is your planning today?

Plans are nothing; planning is everything.

(Dwight Eisenhower)

4 Conquering our mountains

What do you do with your mountains?

All of us, at some time or another, will encounter mountains (impediments, challenges, obstacles, trials, setbacks, disappointments) as we journey through life. How we respond to our mountains matters.

- Do we tend to ignore them (closing our eyes), hoping that if we do not acknowledge them, they will go away?
  - Think about a person who knows they have an illness but fails to go to the doctor to seek treatment.

- Do we climb mountains with the intent of conquering them, coming out victorious, and being a stronger person?
    - I can think of Bernie Marcus and Arthur Blank, who were both fired from Handy Dan and, as a result, went on to create Home Depot.
- Do we seek avoidance to circumvent them in the hope that they will not really affect us?
    - There was this person who had a bad auto accident but came out unscathed. His wife advised him to seek medical care to check for any hidden health issues. He refused, saying he was fine, only to find out several years later that his recurring migraines were the after-effect of the accident.
- Do we try to explode or blow them up, not caring about the fallout or the consequences?
    - This reminds me of a case where a man had a rodent problem in his crawl space and, instead of calling the professionals, decided he could handle this on his own. As a result, he almost burnt his house down. We can remember OJ Simpson, who took matters into his own hands to retrieve some memorabilia that he claimed was stolen. He engaged in a robbery case in 2007. He and a group of men entered a hotel room in Las Vegas to retrieve the items. As a result of this incident, he was convicted of multiple charges, including that of armed robbery.
    - Closer to home, I recalled the time when we had slugs eating our plants. My plans were to get some slug pellets to address the problem. My wife, on the other hand, took matters into her own hands and applied salt around the base of the plants. Sure enough, this killed the slugs, but weeks later, all the plants started dying.

Wisdom is the ability to know which option to choose and the intended outcome to be realized from the choice made.

If the mountain were smooth, you would not be able to climb it.

Crisis does not develop character; it demonstrates character.

5 Change agent or changed agent?

Very often, you will hear the term, "I do not like change." But is this really a true statement? What we do not like are the changes that make us worse off than before. Who would not like to have a positive change in their bank account, in their health, or quality of life?

Change is a constant in our world whether we like it or not and very often does not ask our permission to act. Some changes happen suddenly, others gradually, some without warning, while others are more planned and controlled. Some are within our control, and some are not. What really matters is how we respond to change.

Take some time to better understand the nature of the change. What caused the change? Figure out how the change will affect you. Is there anything you can do to better absorb the change, such as adjusting your attitude, approach or position? Measure the impact of the change and get insight from others who can help you to embrace the change. (Try not to reach out to people who are strongly biased in your favor and will only tell you what you want to hear). Carefully make your decision on how you will respond to the change, always seeking to come out stronger and better from it, not worse.

So, when a change is being introduced, allow time to absorb, digest, or transition to it. Determine how that change can improve the situation you are in. How can I capitalize or benefit from the change? In short, making raisins out of stale grapes or lemonade out of lemons.

There are two types of people in the world: those that enter a room and make things happen and those that come in later and ask what happened?

6 Shadows

Every tree casts a shadow. Influence and its impact on others!

Every tree has a shadow, and we, like trees, have shadows. Our shadows represent the influence or impact we have on others, whether bad or good, intentionally or unintentionally. We, in turn, have been influenced by others: parents, teachers, friends, work colleagues, managers, entertainers, and sports professionals. Influencing is a two-way street. What we do affects the behavior and response of others. Some impacts may be instantaneous, a "flash in the pan," while others are more lasting and sometimes permanent.

As you go through your days, take some time to look at the shadows you cast on how you influence others. Your speech, your conduct, your deportment, your attitudes, your approach, your values, and your differences all contribute to the influence we have on others.

Every great river starts with a drop of water, so let's consciously decide to make incremental changes to leave a positive impact and influence on those we relate to and interact with. Note as you move, your shadow follows you; it falls on all the people around as you move. Let your shadow be a safe place where others feel safe as it falls on them. Take some time to look around and see where you cast your shadow. Who are the people in your shadow? How about the cashier at the retail store, your co-worker and colleague, the waiter at the restaurant, your supervisor at work, your children, your spouse, and your friends?

Your shadow is always with you. What is the shape of your shadow?

Shadows are only created when the light is limited to one side of the object, who is the source of your light?

7 Path of least resistance

We all live in a fast-paced world, and we are constantly being asked to get it done faster and faster, sometimes with the same resources or even less. We are challenged to get it done as quickly as possible, keep up or beat the competition and be the first ones there. The need for speed is the new clarion call.

I remember some years back on a consulting engagement where the consultants were putting in some long hours on a mission-critical project; the client asked why the team was not working through the night. The response was that they had to get some sleep, to which came the response, “Get them to sleep faster.”

This may seem funny, but do we find ourselves caving in to get things done just for expediency, cutting corners, and taking shortcuts as opposed to doing the right thing? We may reach the finish line faster, but at what cost? Have we sacrificed quality, relationships, effectiveness and efficiency in doing so?

So, the next time you have an activity to get done, ask yourself this question: "Am I going to do it in such a way that will cut corners to have some short-term gratification, or will I do it correctly with a more lasting gratification knowing that I did the right thing?"

Taking the path of least resistance is what makes both rivers and men crooked.

8 In the midst of the storm

Yes, let's be honest; we all have encountered storms of different varieties and ferocities in our work and personal lives. Some of these have been self-generated, others have been, well, "thrust upon us."

So, what is our response when caught up in the turmoil of a storm? Is it to seek for the panic button and further exacerbate the situation? Are we making the situation worse by our desperate actions? Better yet, it is to be prepared, knowing that storms are a part of life; expect them. When they do arise, remain calm (breathe slowly) and be confident. Draw on your strengths, reserves and capabilities. Do not make matters worse by throwing up your arms in despair or, worse yet, "punching holes in the boat."

Take time to assess the situation, look at options, consider the alternatives, think and respond rather than just reacting. Seek a map or a lantern (some proven method or a person with proven expertise and competence) to get you through. Above all else, do not press the panic button and try not to congregate with all the other panicking team members on the same side of the boat. That will only cause it to capsize.

We are reminded of the remarkable story of Captain Robert FitzRoy of HMS Beagle. During the ship's second voyage (1831-1836), which famously carried Charles Darwin, FitzRoy demonstrated exceptional navigational skills and leadership. The Beagle faced numerous storms and treacherous conditions while charting the coasts of South America. His ability to keep the ship, crew and passengers safe through these challenges is a testimony to his seamanship and leadership.

Calm seas do not make good captains, but good captains seek calm seas.

9 The power of fear

We all have it, and yes, some of us more so than others. We were not born with it, but over time, we have learned how to cultivate and nurture it. At times, it causes paralysis, it makes us shake uncontrollably, it gives us goose pimples, sweaty palms, and even high blood pressure. Sometimes, it causes us to do crazy things. Yes, we are talking about fear, the perception that some future event will cause us harm, injury or loss in those things that make us safe, valued and comfortable.

Fear is a mental state of mind; outside of our minds, it does not exist. It is a sister to worry and anxiety. Fear can be healthy at times and helps us avoid doing stupid things, but at other times, it is extremely unhealthy, robbing us of energy and the ability to enjoy life. Someone once said **FEAR** is an acronym meaning False Evidence Appearing Real. The point is we do not need to be a victim of fear. When we start replacing those thoughts with memories of success, triumphs and accomplishments, we are driving back fear.

We conquer fear when we look at the positive outcome and how we have dealt with similar situations in the past. We keep fear under control when we share our concerns with others who care. *Fear is like ice cream, have too much of it too quickly, and you will get brain freeze.*

Fear only wins when we allow it to conquer us. Courage is not the absence of fear it is the mastery of it.

10 The eye and the cheek

We have all been in those situations where our best intentions were thrown back at us, where our best efforts were rewarded with ingratitude or even with insult. As we bump into others as we go through life, we will inevitably get the type of negative feedback that can knock us off our rockers. Whoa! Hold on a minute, what was that for?

Sometimes, we are insulted when we are kind, we are not recognized when we believe we should be, we are berated for no apparent reason, and we are intentionally embarrassed in public. In short, other people are just plain mean to us, sometimes for no apparent reason. How we respond to those situations and individuals is a true measure of the type of person we truly are. How about instead of getting even or fighting back, we go above and beyond the norm by showing increased grace and kindness? Instead of fighting for our rights, we forgive the wrong. Instead of whining about how our feelings have been hurt why not recognize the feelings of others and seek to understand where they are coming from? In short, how about turning the other cheek and being prepared for the hit that may occur on that cheek or the other one?

If we only do what is expected of us, then we are no better off than when we came out of the womb; we operate at the same level as our offender. To paraphrase Mahatma Gandhi, "if we take out the offending person's eye every time he takes out ours, then very soon we will all be blind".

We should first take the log out of our eye before attempting to take the speck out of the eye of the other person.

(Jesus)

11 Blaming the darkness

It's really dark in here. How in the world am I to see where I am going, much more see what's in the room?

We have all found ourselves in situations where it seems that there is no way out. We are at a loss as to how to move forward. Our first instinct is to blame the circumstances or those responsible for landing us in this predicament. But as this old Chinese proverb postulates, "instead of blaming the circumstances or situation in which we find ourselves, light a candle."

Groping in the darkness is fraught with danger. We can unintentionally bump into others causing pain. If we are alone in the darkness, we invariably end up colliding with unseen objects, which may harm us.

Lighting a candle allows us to explore other options, how to improve or correct the situation, and how to advance instead of staying stuck in the situation. How to position ourselves for success instead of complaining and adopting a bad attitude. Instilling hope instead of despair.

How does one turn on the light in a dark room? Take the time to take stock of the situation. Check if you have the resources to improve the situation or if there is someone else you can reach out to that can help. Revisit past instances where you successfully addressed similar darkness and apply those techniques if applicable.

So, next time you find yourself in a dark room (whether of your making or not), try and light the candle, or since we are more technically advanced, turn on the flashlight (there is an app for that on your phone). Hopefully, you have working batteries that you have taken with you, and you know where to find them.

Darkness is the absence of light; what is the source of your light?

12 What's in your cup?

If you bump into a person carrying a cup of coffee, we expect that what spills out is coffee, exactly what is in the cup. As we go through our daily trips, we invariably will get bumped by others or we will bump into things or others. Our response, attitude, and disposition to that bump reflect what is in us, that is, what is in our cup.

So, what's in your cup? What comes out when you get bumped? Anger, grace, gentility, humor, guile, humility, pride, arrogance, forgiveness, cursing, blessings, gratitude, ingratitude?

The contents of our cups can sometimes take years to accumulate. Think of ingrained bad habits that only become worse over time. Unfortunately for many of us, we have many ingredients that make up the contents within our cups. Are you quick to get angry when you are offended? Do you readily give people a "piece of your mind" when they rub you the wrong way? Do you celebrate others whose accomplishments outshine yours? Think of that person who got the promotion that you thought you were in line for.

One of the places where we see people spilling hot, steaming beverages on others is on our roadways. You continue to hear repeated stories of people in road rage incidents, where, at times, people are shot for what seems the slightest offense.

How do you know what's inside your cup? Just ask others around you, the people you relate to on a regular basis. Maybe this is an exercise you do on your birthday. If you do discover that the content of your cup is usually unsavory, acknowledge this, be willing to change and take meaningful steps to reduce and remove the unhealthy content. Remember, "what's down in the well comes up in the bucket".

Our beliefs shape our behavior. As a person thinks, so he is. Whatsoever things are true, whatsoever things are honest, whatsoever things are just, whatsoever things are pure, whatsoever things are lovely, whatsoever things are of good report, think on these things.

A person is defined not by what goes into him but by what comes out of him – (Jesus).

13 Cleaning cobwebs versus killing spiders

My daughter has a genuine fear of spiders; I guess you would call her an arachnophobe. She will not go near the spiders but has no fear of cleaning up their webs once she is assured the spiders are nowhere to be seen.

How odd, you say? But how many of us are like her? Instead of addressing the source of the issue, we focus more time and energy on addressing the symptoms, trying to clean up the effects of the cause. Think about your personal (health, financial) situations, relationships, and work settings; do you find yourself focusing on the cobwebs, or do you take the time to identify the spiders and deal with them? And believe me, some spiders do spin their webs very fast, leaving their sticky, gooey threads behind to get the next victim.

Take the time to go beyond the symptoms. Use the 5-whys root cause analysis, which for every answer seeks to find the cause contributing to this until you get to the primary cause of the problem. Correctly size up the cause and seek help if you know your limitations to deal effectively with it. Someone who has expertise in that area is usually a good starting point, especially if the underlying cause of the problem is highly impactful.

1. Identify the problem: Clearly state the problem you are facing.
2. Ask, "Why?": Ask why the problem occurred and write down the answer.
3. Repeat: Ask "Why?" again based on the previous answer. Continue this process until you have asked "Why?" five times.
4. Identify the root cause: By the fifth "Why?" you should have uncovered the root cause of the problem.
5. Take action: Develop corrective actions to address the root cause and prevent recurrence of the problem.

(Take some time and watch a spider at work. My preferred times are outdoors at dusk. You will see what I am talking about: speed, agility, and precision in fluid motion.)

What is more amazing is that some of us get entangled in the cobwebs during the cleaning process. So, when next you are seeking to remediate, improve, or ameliorate a situation, ask yourself, "Am I just treating the symptoms, or am I really addressing the root cause?" Am I just cleaning up the cobwebs and allowing the spiders to go free to make even more cobwebs, or am I really getting rid of the spiders?

You cannot clean the inside by cleaning the outside.

14 Tops and bottoms

Have you ever seen a mountain without a bottom? Imagine the pyramids without a base. We tend to admire successful achievers who seem to be at the top or come out on top. But as we all know, we live in an interconnected and highly interdependent world.

Our successes and accomplishments are not ours alone but are the result of many others who work behind the scenes to help us to be successful. Those who have laid the foundation and bear the brunt of the weight for us to come out on top. Think of great leaders who represent the epitome of achievement in their fields (Jeff Bezos, Stephen Jobs, Henry Ford, Abraham Lincoln, Warren Buffet, Christopher Columbus et al); their achievements were made possible by the support they received from those who worked for them or who served them in lower levels or at the bottom.

Those at the top may have more responsibilities in line with their position, but this in no way should discount the work of those serving under them who make their position important.

Think of a general without having an army or troops to command. Corporate America, by its very nature, runs on a hierarchical work model. In earlier times, when unions were commonplace, as those at the bottom were not well looked after, a strike would inevitably bring the company to a halt. In short, the workers were saying you Mr. Company manager or president, may be on top, but we are the ones who keep your there.

So, if you are sitting at the top, ask yourself who is at the bottom providing the support? Think of those who prepared the meals providing the sustenance we needed, fellow team members who put in some long hours to make the project deadline. Think of that person who had to forego personal commitments to make us successful. In short, let us take the time to acknowledge those who serve quietly behind the scenes, remembering that there is no "I" in SUCCESS, and there can be no "top" without a "bottom." Remember, o*thers help us to get where we are today.*

So, if you are at the top, ask yourself who provides the basis for your success?

15 Digging holes

As humans, we are endowed with intellect and the ability to reason, yet we sometimes end up doing things that we look at later and say, “What in the world was I thinking?” I remember one occasion as a child my friends and I wanted to see how deep a hole we could dig. Yes, we wanted to see if it was possible to get to the center of the earth.

So, we got our shovels and other digging implements and started digging. Well, before you knew it, we had a nice hole. Soon, we realized that we had a problem we had not thought of before. As we dug deeper, we were unable to throw the displaced earth completely out of the hole. In fact, the bigger kids could throw some of the dirt out, but invariably, it started raining back into the hole and getting into our hair, eyes and into our clothes. We discovered that the deeper we dug, the harder it became to get rid of the displaced earth, and worse yet, the earth was making us filthy.

And now here we are as adults, and we are still digging holes, at times not knowing when to stop. Just as children, we quickly find out that the deeper we dig ourselves in, the harder it is to get rid of the dirt and very often, it smears us. Not only does it become harder to get rid of, but as the hole gets deeper, it becomes harder to get out of it. So, the advice is when you realize that your digging is only making matters worse stop digging.

Count and cut your losses and move on. It will not get better by digging deeper or longer. And something I forgot to mention, we had to pay the price for the dirty clothes we brought home to our parents. So, when you see others digging holes, let them know the damage they are doing to themselves and others when they throw the displaced dirt out of the hole. The dirt must fall somewhere. *It is exceedingly difficult to dig yourself out of a hole.*

When you throw dirt from the hole you are digging, check your hands to see how dirty they are.

16 When emotion is high, cognition is low

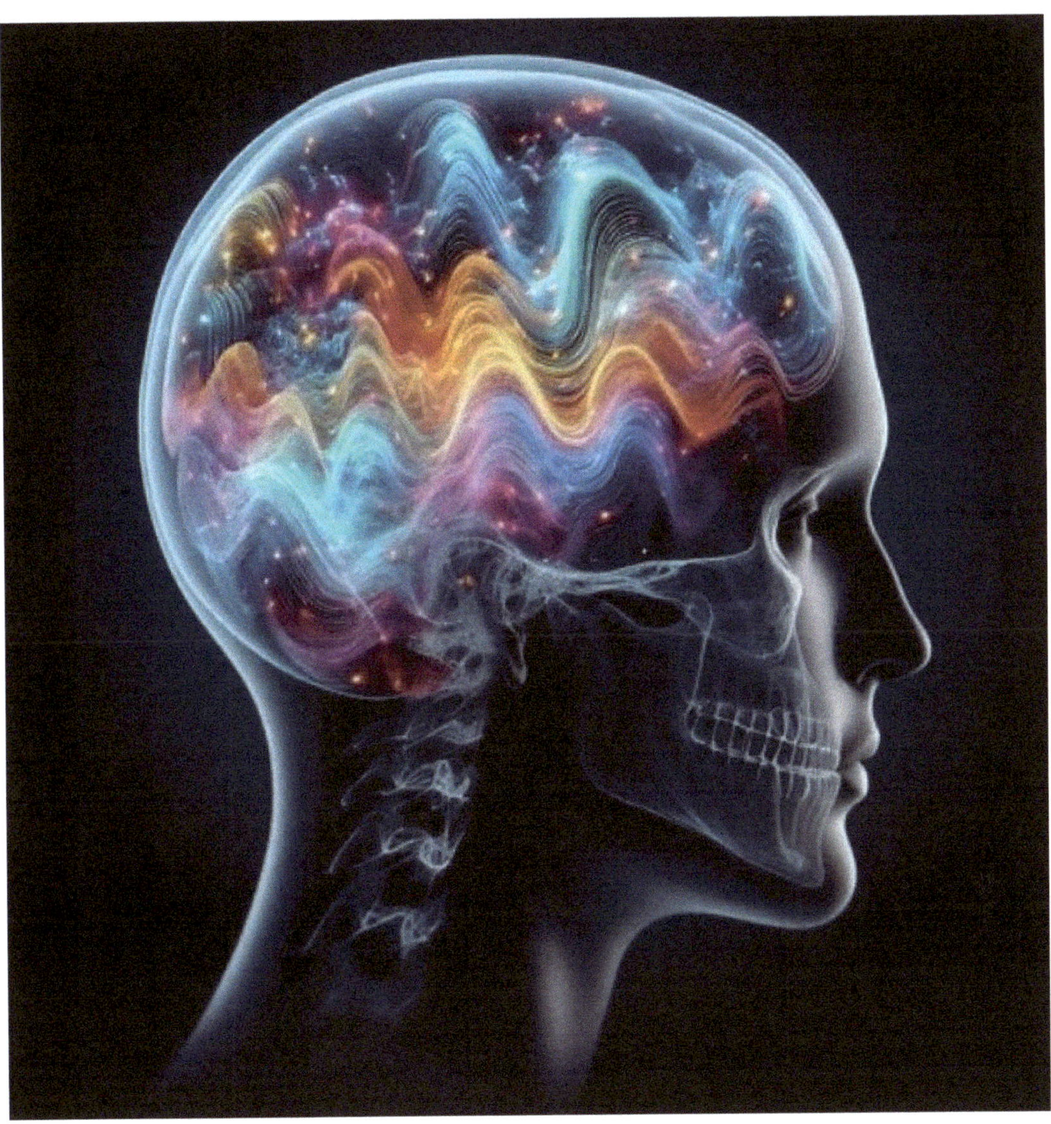

My wife said that to me recently after someone we knew in the height of some emotional excitement made a commitment that he later regretted when he was more sedated.

Yes, funny as it sounds, when we are emotionally high-strung, whether with joy, pleasure, fear, pain, or anger, our ability to reason and make sound decisions takes the back seat. It seems that both faculties cannot perform optimally at the same time. So, we need to be cautious if our emotional temperature is high (whether with pleasure, pain, or anger) not to make commitments, statements, or responses that may cause more harm than good. Here, then, is a breakdown of the paradigm.

1. **Emotional Overload**: When we experience strong emotions like anger, fear, or excitement, our brain's emotional center (the amygdala) can become highly active.

2. **Cognitive Impairment:** This heightened emotional state can interfere with the functioning of the prefrontal cortex, the part of the brain responsible for logical thinking, decision-making, and self-control.

3. **Reduced Rationality**: As a result, our ability to process information, think critically, and make sound decisions can be compromised. We might act impulsively or make choices we wouldn't normally make if we were calm.

The problem is, we may know to do the right thing when going into a situation, but then we fall victim to the law. We forget this when we are caught up in the emotional heat of the moment.

So, what to do when this happens? Raise the sign: "Anything I say or do when my emotions are high should not be used against me when my emotions are unsettled." In other words, seek to gain control of your emotions, slow down, walk away, and take five.

I only trust my intellect when my emotions tell me to.

17 Don't slam the door. Don'ts do not tell us what to do

SLAM! And then the inevitable shout from the father in a burst of anguish: "How many times do I have to tell you? DON'T SLAM THE DOOR!!" An innocuous statement, you say, but how many times do we find ourselves in the same situation? We repeatedly tell people how "not" to do something and then become bewildered when they fail to do what we want. Maybe the problem is not so much with the person on the other end, failing to obey or execute our instructions, but rather with us and the instructions we provide. My wife brought this to my attention recently, "instead of telling our son not to slam the door, tell him to close the door gently," she said.

The focus of the instruction changed from "DO NOT" to "DO." Now, the instructions are more positive and intentional; action can follow now that there is a clear expectation of what to do rather than what not to do. Somehow, our brains respond more favorably to do-s than don'ts. We all experience that with young children; tell them not to do something, and we are surprised that they do just the opposite, and we wonder aloud what their problem is.

So, next time you want someone to change a behavior do not (did I just say that) communicate the negative aspect of the instruction, but rather the positive do of the instruction. That is, do tell them what action needs to be taken to achieve the desired results or outcomes.

PS. Don't tell me that this is obvious, and we don't need to be told this.

18 Learning from others who disagree with us

Human nature is a funny thing, and it often does not always work in our best interest. We are driven to associate with people who have similar interests as we do; we call these biases.

Very often, when we have disagreements with others, we rally around those who we know will support our position and viewpoint. Therein lies the danger. We tend to learn far more from people who disagree with us rather than those who agree with us.

Strange, you say, but think about this for a while. If the people we listen to tend to echo and reflect our thoughts and viewpoints, no new insight is added. However, if others do disagree with us and we are mature enough, we will consider their point of view and give it due consideration. In so doing, we see things from different perspectives and, more importantly, open ourselves up to learning new things.

Think of the common analogy of the three blind men and the elephant; if the person who is feeling the trunk and deems it a tree only surrounds himself with people who have the same position, what is there to learn? However, if he takes into consideration the different viewpoints of the person who is touching the tail and the other who is touching the ear, he may recognize that there is more to this object than just a trunk.

So, be open to viewpoints and positions different from yours, disarm your ego, and realize that life is not just about us but really taking input from all those around us to make worthwhile and wholesome decisions.

A person only gets stronger by lifting weights that oppose his efforts.

19 Promising versus planning

We all have noble intentions of doing what is asked of us. Our default response very often when asked to do something for someone else is that we will do so. When pressed, we declare with such amplified certainty, "I promise to…." Think about that for a while. How often have you been in situations where another has pressed you to fulfill some obligation, and the response is, "I promise to.."

Well, what we have all discovered is that we are terrible at keeping promises. Even when well-intentioned, disruptions, events, and life get in the way that prevents us from honoring those promises. I learned this lesson early as a young father when my daughter would ask me to do some things with her, and my response would be, "I promise to….."

Unfortunately, due to circumstances outside of my control, I failed to honor that promise, which, in turn, eroded her trust in me as a father. I could not keep my word. So, after some careful reflection and soul searching, I promised (pun intended) myself I would no longer make promises; instead, my response would be "I plan on ….." or "Let us plan on doing…" The fact of the matter is when we make promises, we have very little control over events or circumstances that could derail us from keeping those promises.

Life incidents get in the way of us fulfilling those promises. Traffic congestion, health issues, tragedies, and a myriad of other things more often than not derail our best intentions of keeping our promises. So, not being a wimp, I now take a more practical approach by saying, "I am planning on getting this done." Taking this mindset prevents us from artificially setting expectations that, in turn, ruin our credibility and trust with others and ourselves when we fail to deliver.

The road to hell is paved with many good intentions. (Bernard of Clairvaux)

20 Constructive confrontation is better than artificial harmony

Life, for the most part, consists of people interacting with people, sharing ideas, emotions, services and so on. Inevitably, we will encounter unfilled expectations, hurt, anguish, joy, pain, and remorse in relationships. However, most people fear having a confrontation with another person, especially when they think it may impair the relationship. For that reason, they will avoid the "elephant in the room," put on blinders and behave as if everything is O.K. Constructive confrontation takes courage.

Technically, we pretend to get along, living artificial lives, not being honest and true. More energy and anxiety are expended when we practice artificial harmony, avoiding land mines. A better way to have a more wholesome relationship is to confront the situation in a positive and constructive manner. Get to the core of the issue and work on ways to improve.

Steps for positive confrontation

1. Learn to separate your emotions from the situation.
2. Stick to the important points, separate facts from opinions, and avoid assumptions.
3. Make your point and give the other person space and time to respond. Listen with the intent to hear clearly what is being communicated.
4. Check for misunderstanding and clarify motive and intention.
5. Based on the magnitude of the situation, do it in person or have a neutral person present.
6. Be respectful.
7. Avoid blame and finger-pointing, judgmental disposition or attitude.
8. Suggest a solution and strive for a positive outcome.

Doing nothing is not an option. Very often, we discover that what originally appeared to be an elephant turned out to be an ant.

Wine is only one of the few things that get better with age.

21 Cutting down the coconut tree

The following is a true story recounted to me by a friend who lived in the Caribbean. She was getting ready to run some errands when some neighborhood boys approached her as she was preparing to drive off. They wanted to know if she would allow them to pick some of the coconuts growing on the tree in her backyard. Coconut trees can grow upwards of 20 feet tall or more and produce coconuts in clumps based on the particular species. Her coconut tree was rather tall and had been there for over 15 years.

The coconut has an inner white cream-like jelly, and when it is near maturity, the interior is filled with a thirst-quenching liquid commonly known as coconut water, which is not to be confused with coconut milk, which is the liquid extracted from the hardened white jelly. She told them they could and left to attend to her errands. However, when she returned, to her great dismay, she did not see the coconut tree. She ran to the back of the house, and there, like a slaughtered animal lying in its death throe, was the coconut tree, stripped clean of all its coconuts. She could not believe that these boys would cut the coconut tree down, entirely removing its productivity just to get a few coconuts.

What does cutting your coconut tree look like?

- Destroying the source of income through foolish acts.
- Cutting off those who have been influential in your advances in life.
- Being unkind to those who have helped you in tough times.

So, as we go about our journey and enjoy the "fruits" of living, we need to ask the question: Are we cutting down our "coconut trees"?

He who cuts off his foot should not complain he has no toes.

22 ANTS versus PETS

Most, if not all, of us have ants and sometimes pets in our homes. Ants are uninvited guests. It does not matter about the state or the age of the home; these seemingly indomitable pests invariably show up very often without warning. Pets, on the other hand, are the result of deliberate and intentional choices based on an expressed desire to invest in something that will result in an enhanced quality of life (most of the time). Pets do require ongoing dedicated maintenance and support.

Just as a home has both ants and pets, our mental homes also have ANTs and PETs. ANTs in the mental home are what we call Automatic Negative Thoughts (courtesy of Dr. Daniel Amen). These readily manifest themselves without warning. They come in different varieties and shapes: for example, worry ANT- thoughts centered on worrying that things will not turn out well; lazy ANT- these thoughts are centered on "it will not work"; failure ANT: "This has been tried before, it is going to fail;" killer ANT- "you know that it will not live, it will die;" fear ANT- "I am afraid it is not going to…"

These ANTs are usually the first mental responses we generate or conjure when going through different situations, conditions, or opportunities. PETs, on the other hand, are Positive, Edifying Thoughts that require conscious effort and intent to be developed. Like true pets, they must be cultivated, trained, and cared for. PETs encourage others, look on the bright side, see beneficial outcomes and opportunities, are uplifting, and, at the end of the day, give hope. So, decide which you would rather have, destructive, biting ANTs or beneficial, loving PETs?

Whatsoever things are true, of good report, honest and uplifting, think about these things. (The Bible)

23 Running the race at the right pace

The 2013 IAAF World Championship held in Moscow from August 12-16 had some inspirational highlights, especially in some of the track events. In one of the long-distance races (10,000 meters if my memory serves me correctly), one runner went out in front, setting a hectic pace from the get-go, but ended the race in almost the last position, falling to the ground in the process. The eventual winner paced herself throughout the race, slowly but ever surely making ground on the other competitors until in the final 400 meters when she kicked it into high gear and won the race comfortably.

Another highlight was from the 100 and 200-meter champion Shelly-Ann Fraser-Pryce. After winning the 200 meters, she shared that she did not like running the 200 meters. However, at the start of the season, she committed and challenged herself to overcome that mental block and focus her training on mastering the running of the 200 meters. Additionally, her coach played a significant role in getting her to train more effectively to finish the race strong, as in the past, she would "fly" through the first 100 meters but then wane on the last 100 meters. That being said, here are some pointers for us to consider as we run the race that is set for us.

1. **Lose the weight**. Lose the excess baggage and those things that readily weigh us down. Negative attitudes and thoughts (ANTs), negative memories, worries, and concerns outside of our control.

2. **Get rid of parasitic behaviors.** These are unproductive behaviors we perform that consume our energy and resources unnecessarily. These behaviors tend to linger, are hard to give up, and are very destructive to goal achievement. They are like the slow leak that drains and requires more energy to push ahead. So, energy is expended on the parasitic behavior rather than on the productive behavior of accomplishing the goal.

3. **Run to endure.** Keep the goal in mind. Keep focused on the finish line. Set a pace that is realistic in getting to the tape safely. If you get distracted or get off course, look out for those who are running and follow them (assuming they are going in the same direction and have similar goals). Find a champion/coach who has already run and finished their race and emulate the techniques that will work best for you!

24 Fact versus truth

If enough people believe the same thing, it becomes a fact. For example, the sun rises in the east is a common fact. If a person challenges the commonly held belief or fact, he is very often deemed a lunatic or a fool. Herein lies the problem: we use opinions, interpretations, and common observations over time to create facts that we assert as truths. These truths are things we sometimes hold dear and would never relinquish. (There is currently an insurance ad running that shows how one individual uses a mass media channel: "the internet," to shape her beliefs and, ultimately, her conduct). However, not all facts are truth.

Truths are absolute. Truth: The earth rotates on its axis, giving the impression that the sun is moving; the sun technically does not rise or set. Think Copernicus. Much of science and the judicial system are centered on trying to determine facts to reveal truth to shape understanding, actions, and outcomes. In the same way, we should exercise care in what we deem to be truth and how we act on this. And by the way, there is no such thing as an alternative fact unless you believe this to be true.

Here are some things to consider:

- Truth is absolute - it is what it is.
- Facts are relative – they may change over time and are based on commonly held beliefs, interpretations, and experiences.
- Verify facts.
- Not all facts are truth, and not all truth is fact; know the difference.
- Seek out the truth - not all that glitters is gold.

A fact to a person remains their truth until it is changed.

25 How far is our vision?

All of us have a vision of ourselves and others. The question that must be asked is, "how accurate is that vision?" When we look at ourselves or others, what do we see? Think about this for a minute, for us to fully see ourselves, we look in a mirror. We actually see an image (reflection of the object) of ourselves, not actually the real object itself.

However, when we look at others, we are looking at the real object. So, which do you think provides a more accurate representation of the vision of ourselves - the image or the object? When we look at ourselves through mirrors, we tend to be handicapped. We cannot see our back. How clean is the mirror? Is this a full-length mirror? Can the mirror allow us to see our back while at the same time seeing our front? Worse yet, what if our vision is blurred? I have a beam (4X4 piece of lumber) in my eye that I am actively working on reducing to improve my vision so that I can have greater clarity of my image. So, as you can see, our vision of ourselves will always be marred by impediments, limitations, and imperfections in our "eyesight" and the "quality" of the mirror.

People with whom we interact on a more regular basis are in a better position to provide us with a more authentic and less flawed vision of ourselves. They can readily see us in all dimensions, under different situations, and in a variety of settings and conditions, giving them increased field depth and width of vision of us. So, going forward, decide which vision you would like to have of yourself, an image or the object of who you are. And if you must rely solely on your mirror, ask yourself this question: when was the last time you had it cleaned, or better yet, when was the last time you had your "eyesight" checked?

Vision, without it, the people perish – (The Bible.)

26 Dictators are created by default

Most, if not all of us, resent bullies and dictators, those who believe they are more important than the rest of God's creation. However, I have discovered that bullies and dictators are monsters that we create. Yes, we are responsible for their creation. And yet, you say that cannot be. But think about it: when you allow another person's selfish demands or desires to go unchecked, you are giving them the right and freedom to advance their position.

We mostly want to have stable and peaceful relationships with others and, at times, are willing to make concessions. However, we need to draw lines when behaviors are unacceptable and our turfs are being violated. Think about the bully at school: you give him an inch, he takes a foot; you then give him a foot, and he takes over the yard. (Maybe you really should have given him the real foot). Childhood bullies who do not change invariably become adult dictators. They are like Kudzu or weeds in a garden. If you do not attempt to contain their bad behavior and growth in the early stages, they will eventually, ever so gradually, take over. And what is most amazing is that once the dictators are established, they become more difficult to contain and control.

So, as you go through life, make sure you are not capitulating to others and, in so doing, create dictators. Stand your ground to those who want to ride roughshod over you. Do not succumb to their pressure and negative influence. Push back. Hold the line. Guard your integrity and honor. Hold them accountable for their actions.

The child who throws a temper tantrum at his parents because they failed to do what he wants but then gives in to "keep the peace" should not wonder that the child now a teen is irascible and uncontrollable.

People who are easily intimidated when asked to jump do not ask how high; rather, they ask when to come down.

27 It's the small things in life that get you

A professor was addressing his students. The topic was about the fact that "details count." He asked this question: "How many people have ever been bitten by an elephant?" Puzzled, his students said none of them had, and some shook their heads to indicate they never had. Then he continued, "How many people have been bitten by a dog?" This time, quite a few hands went up. He paused for a few seconds and asked, "How many have been bitten by mosquitoes?" This time, all hands went up.

He said, "The moral of the story is - it is the little things that get you."

So, very often, we focus on the big things, and we attempt to go after the "big" ones. What if, however, we tried to address the "small" things one at a time? In other words, trying to get rid of those pesky mosquitoes.

Learning how to manage our finances when we have limited resources, training our bodies to eat well, to get enough rest. Taking walks and doing 15 - 30 minutes daily exercises to enhance the long-term viability of our health. Laughing instead of getting upset over minor things. In short, take little steps now to cover the longer distance of the journey.

Do you know what your elephant is versus your mosquito? Which is easier to address? Quite obviously, the mosquito. So, as we continue the journey, try to get your mosquitoes conquered first.

28 Who is on the other end of your spoon?

Human beings are a strange and paradoxical species. We enjoy being together and creating groups with common interests and values, but we invariably spend more energy and effort doing things that destroy the very things we want to preserve. When we collectively have the same goals, values and desires in mind, we pull together to make it happen. We forgive errors, we encourage others, we help others. In short, we live out the values of teamwork. "All for one and one for all," as Alexandre Dumas trumpeted in his Musketeers novels. However, in the next vein, it is not surprising to find ourselves in an adversarial position with others. We refuse to contribute, or when we do, we do so sparingly; we bear grudges against others, we discourage, and we scandalize. Instead of working together to advance a common cause, we turn on each other and become cannibalistic in our behavior.

Think of this story: a man had a dream where he first visited hell and noticed that the people there were seated at a table, all with long spoons, trying to drink their soup. However, the scene was one of chaos, fighting with tempers flaring. Some were poking each other with their spoons, trying to feed themselves; fights broke out, the spoons were too long, and hence many of the people were knocking over the bowls of soup, jabbing their neighbors with the spoons. There you have it, hell in motion.

The next part of his dream took him to heaven, where again he saw a table with people seated around using the same long spoons as the people in hell. However, they were all peacefully drinking their soup. What made the difference? Each person sitting across from each other took turns feeding each other with their long spoons. Here was togetherness in action. Each helping the other. So, as you go through your journey, ask yourself: what am I doing with my spoon? Who is on the other end?

Togetherness at its best is unbeatable; togetherness at its worst is unbearable.

29 Sound cannot travel in a vacuum

This may not be common knowledge, but sound cannot travel in a vacuum. Sound travels as waves and needs matter (molecules) to transmit the signal. You say what is the significance of that to me? Much of our lives entail interacting and communicating with others. For better or for worse, we are not always the best at communicating. For a long while, I mistakenly thought that the importance of communication was getting my intentions and points across to the other person. If I had confirmation that this was done effectively, I was satisfied in knowing that I was successful with my communication. But I had a recent wake-up call where, as part of a program I was participating in, I was made aware that effective communication should result in mutual understanding. That is, both parties must have a good understanding of each other's position, intentions, and thoughts at the end of the exchange.

For effective communication to occur, several components must be present: 1) the sender/transmitter, 2) the message, 3) the method/ medium in which the message is transmitted, and 4) the receiver. As we communicate, we need to be aware of these key elements: As the sender, are we clear and concise? Are we distracted? Are we disorganized? Are we allowing time for the receiver to absorb and process the message? Are we using a common language? Is the timing correct? Are we using the right tones? Are we emotionally distraught? Is our body language, our attitudes, and disposition supporting the message? What about the message: is it clear and simple in a language that the receiver can easily understand? Next, the medium and method in which the message is communicated; is the medium appropriate? Can a song do instead of a narrative? Are we using emails when face-to-face communication can work better? Are we hiding behind social media when a chat over lunch will do? Is it better to act out than to write it out? Are we shouting when a whisper will suffice? Finally, as the receiver, are we engaged, are we pre-occupied or distracted with other things? Are we listening? Are we paying attention? Are we providing positive feedback that we understand or do not understand? Are we tired? Are we taking the time to process, digest, and absorb the information? So, if you want to know that your communication is effective, find out how much vacuum was between you and the other person(s).

Silence is not the absence of sound; rather, it is the inability to hear.

30 Mind reading, telepathy and expectations

We rise and fall based on how our expectations turn out. All of us live by expectations in one form or another. An expectation is essentially an outcome or behavior we would like to see happen or should occur. As we go through life, we set expectations of ourselves, of others, of systems, of organizations. We expect that when we wake up, we will be able to get out of bed; we expect that when we turn the key in the car, it will start; we expect that our houses will be intact when we return home; we expect to get paid on a certain date, we expect others to know what we like and need. We expect that our friends will remember our birthdays.

When our realities fail to align with our expectations, we can become disappointed, frustrated, and angry and often demonstrate negative emotional responses. The measure of our response (positive or negative), attitude, and reaction are directly proportional to the magnitude of the gap between our expectations and the reality of the situation. Very often, these expectation gaps result from failure to effectively communicate our expectations to others, having unrealistic expectations, having dated expectations that are no longer relevant, and others not knowing our expectations.

So, as you go through your journey, ask yourself these questions: are my expectations realistic and practical? Do others clearly know and understand my expectations of them and of myself? Are my expectations relevant?

Also, remember if you fail to set expectations with others, they will set their own for you and manage towards that. We should set expectations, get agreement, and then manage to meet those expectations.

Hope deferred makes the heart sick, but the fulfillment of expectation brings joy – (The Bible).

31 Confidence

Confidence may be defined to be the positive expectation for a favorable outcome. Self-confidence is rooted in our beliefs that our abilities, competencies, knowledge, track record, and resources to make things happen will produce a favorable outcome. When our confidence levels are high, we almost have a feeling of invincibility and can take on just about any challenge. Our confidence is contagious and very often can influence others in our spheres of influence. If our confidence levels are low, then we emit and radiate negativism, which tends to drain and stifle hope. On the other hand, when our confidence levels are high, we inspire others to excel and go beyond the norm.

High confidence levels give rise to courage, increased energy, and actions to produce favorable outcomes. The sad part about confidence is that we, too, are recipients of other people's confidence emissions. We can be carried in the wake of their confidence levels, whether high or low. People are less likely to follow people who are lacking in confidence. A high confidence level gives us the added impetus to succeed despite the odds; it allows us to silence the nay-sayers and do more than others may think.

Some words of caution.

Success breeds confidence, and over time, if success is not checked and our confidences are allowed to run rabid, it can, in turn, lead to emotional exuberance or arrogance in our behavior and attitudes. Our egos tend to swell, and we start to believe that we are invincible and cannot fail (think of a cat believing it can attack an eagle). So, as we go through our journey, it is always good to check our confidence levels. How much are we allowing the confidence of others, organizations, and systems to affect us? How much are we using our confidence levels to inspire self-accomplishment and others to excel as well?

Confidence allows us to weather storms when the umbrellas are missing.

32 Memories

There are lots of things we take for granted, and without them, life would be very difficult. One of the most important and often overlooked essentials for life is memory. Just think about that for a minute and let that soak in. Without memory, we would not know colors, and we would not be able to speak (we would not remember what words or letters meant and not know our names). Without memory, human society could not advance. We would not remember what is poisonous or harmful, so we would just repeat the event and suffer the consequences repeatedly.

Memories allow us to understand danger and take protective actions; memories allow us to build ideas and generate thoughts. The fact that we have memories allows us to know each other, to develop education, to drive cars, to build, to read, to write, to know who our parents are.

Can you imagine if we had no memory, we would not know how to find our way home? Actually, we would not know where home is. The value of memory is most apparent when we encounter those suffering from dementia and Alzheimer's disease, forgetting their names, how to dress, how to speak, how to eat and even worse, their loved ones.

So, as you continue the journey, remember to be very appreciative of your memory and exercise it to keep it active and functional. The fact that you can read this at all is attributable to memory.

We only realize memory is important when it is lost and we cannot remember what it is.

33 Self-esteem

Self-esteem is a powerful agent in how we behave. Self-esteem may be defined as the level of confidence and sense of worth a person has in their own abilities and value. It entails how a person values himself in terms of their strengths, weaknesses, and overall self-worth . When self-esteem is low, the ego is high, and when self-esteem is high, the ego is low; these are inversely proportional to each other. People with high self-esteem do not need to prove themselves.

Low self-esteem says it is all about me; high self-esteem says it's more about others and less about me. Low self-esteem focuses on "me," "my," and "I." High self-esteem focuses on "us" and "we." Low self-esteem says, "I need to be praised for my efforts and accomplishments"; high self-esteem says, "we praise the team for its efforts and accomplishments." Low self-esteem draws attention to self, and high self-esteem champions the causes and benefits to others. Low self-esteem does not accept culpability for failures, seeks scapegoats, and tends to blame others.

High self-esteem accepts ownership for failures and mistakes and seeks ways to improve. People with high self-esteem tend to demonstrate the following traits.

1. **Positive self-regard**: Hold themselves in positive regard, appreciating their strengths and accepting their weaknesses.

2. **Resilient and intrepid**: Are emotionally strong and can handle setbacks without letting them affect their overall self-worth. They bounce back when things go awry.

3. **Goal-oriented**: Set realistic goals and work towards achieving them, which helps build confidence and a sense of accomplishment.

4. **Self-respect**: Have a strong sense of self-respect and maintain healthy guard rails in relationships.

5. **Optimism:** Tends to envisage outcomes as successes rather than failures and is willing to take calculated risks.

6. **Perspective**: Manage disappointments and successes in perspective.

7. **Principled**: Are guided by strong principles and core values, which provide a blueprint for their life.

8. **Self-caring:** Taking care of themselves physically, mentally, emotionally, and spiritually.

9. **Confident and assured**: Have confidence in their abilities and are not easily shaken by negative criticism or failures.

We have become the people our parents warned us about.

34 The takers

I have discovered in life that there are five types of people, who I will call takers. Well, the last time I checked, this is what I saw:

1. The RISKTAKER - that person is willing to take risks, try out new things, and explore alternate options. Their mantra: "You cannot win if you do not play."

2. The OVERTAKER - that person comes on the scene with a can-do attitude and is willing to take over and move everything forward. Every impediment is a challenge and an opportunity to show that they can get it done. Their mantra: "Get out of the way or get rolled over."

3. The CARETAKER - that person manages the status quo. They only need to be told what to do, and they are content with doing just that, no more and no less. They maintain the shop.

4. The MISTAKER - that person lives to provide excuses for things done wrong or failures. They lack accountability and readily blame outcomes on accidents and errors. “Oops, that was a mistake; my bad.”

5. The UNDERTAKER - that person sees the negative in every situation. Everything will fail; they see the glass not as half full but with a crack and the fluid leaking out. Their mantra is “That will not work, that has been tried before, this is the way we have always done it.”

Not all takers are created equal, take your pick.

35 How sharp is your axe blade?

If the blade of your axe is not sharp, then you will expend more effort in getting your chopping done.

Many of us, as we do work, tend to just keep at it, wondering at the end of the day or sometime later why we are so tired and exhausted. Very often, this can be a result of burn-out. Our axe blades have become dull. We need to take the time to re-charge, "to sharpen the blade," before going on. All together, we believe that putting in long hours without adequate rest and recuperation makes us effective. Yes, we can be effective (doing the right things) but end up being inefficient (not doing things well).

We sometimes get married to our processes and procedures, defending them that this is the way we have always done things, not taking into consideration that those processes and procedures may need to be overhauled.

So, as you go about cutting your trees, remember to check the sharpness of your blade.

Some steps to sharpening your axe blade.

1. Take timely breaks from work during the course of the day.
2. Inject some levity into your life, laugh a little, and let your hair down now and again.
3. Get adequate sleep (7-8 hours).
4. Keep your body healthy with regular exercise, at least 15 minutes daily.
5. Develop and maintain positive social relationships.
6. Maintain, develop and protect your spiritual health and well-being.
7. Eat well, having a balanced diet with fruits, vegetables, reduced processed food and added sugars, including artificial sweeteners.
8. Learn something new and keep your mind active and engaged. Be willing to accept other ways of doing things without compromising the desired outcome.
9. Go on a relaxing vacation.

Man who says it cannot be done should not stand in the way of man getting it done. (Old Chinese proverb).

36 Trees are known by the fruits they bear

You can readily know the type of tree by the fruit it bears. We know pear trees because they bear pears, not oranges. In a similar way, we are very much like trees, and the fruit we bear will tell others who we are. The weather or elements do not redefine a tree; a pear tree is still a pear tree, no matter whether it rains, snows or there is a drought. One of the most telling fruits we can bear is gratitude. For us to become trees of gratitude, we should not allow external circumstances to redefine who we are. Our attitudes of gratitude should not be driven by external conditions or circumstances but rather by our internal convictions, principles and values. If we only express gratitude when things go well, then we will become the most miserable people on the earth.

Expressing thanks and appreciation to others allows us to leave a little bit of ourselves with them. As human beings, we all have a desire to feel appreciated and valued, so as we go through our journey, let us take a few moments to express thanks to others.

- Thanks to those who put up with us despite our many faults and shortcomings.
- Thanks to those who listen to us when we get tired of listening to ourselves.
- Thanks to those who trust us even though we let them down and disappoint them and ourselves.
- Thanks to those who tell us the truth, even when it is a hard pill to swallow.
- Thanks to those who invest in us, we may grow and mature.
- Thanks to those who trust us to do our part.
- Thanks to those who work behind the scenes to make life better for us.

We cultivate the things we celebrate; let us cultivate an attitude of gratitude.

37 What do you do with your grain of sand?

Life for most of us entails encountering incidents, people, or events that are sometimes very irritating or annoying. The way we respond and react to these "irritants" will reveal our true character and the inner fabric of who we are.

We are no different from the oyster that must deal with "irritants" such as a rock particle or a sand grain that gets into its shell. When such an irritant gets into the shell of the oyster, it secretes a liquid (nacre) that covers the irritating particle in layers over time, making it smoother and smoother. The net effect of this action is the production of a pearl that is laced with intrinsic beauty and becomes priceless to those who know its value.

We have the same opportunity to "respond" to our irritants. At the end of the day, do we produce pearls, or do we allow the irritants to get the better of us, leaving us worse off than before? We are the only ones solely responsible for our responses or reactions to situations.

Turning our irritants into pearls:

1. Look for any positive outcome that can be realized from the situation.
2. Take a proactive stance to learn from the situation rather than just complaining.
3. Instead of focusing on ourselves and having pity parties, serve others, especially those who cannot repay us. How about having a party for them?
4. Get rid of any anger, bitterness, ill-feeling and adjust your perspective to make a positive difference.

(Note: Pearls usually take an average of 3 years to reach their full size, no wonder a pearl necklace costs what it does.)

Hardships are opportunities for us to develop solid character.

38 Who are your teachers - bad behavior should not?

I had a most interesting revelation recently. My son was getting ready to move into his newly purchased home. He was highly ecstatic about this and set his moving date. He had invited some of his friends to assist with the move, even though, as his parents, we thought it best for him to use professional movers. (He had several heavy pieces of furniture to move, which he had previously acquired and was in storage in our basement.) Well, my wife, being the smartest one in the family, decided that she would have a back-up plan in place and arranged for the professional movers to be on hand just in case my son's friends could not make it. Well, again, we now know why wives and mothers are the smartest of all God's creations.

On the fateful day of the move, none of my son's friends showed up, so my wife's contingency plan was flawlessly executed, with the professional movers saving the day. The following Saturday, we wanted to help our son "set up house," but he informed us that he would not be at home. His reason is that he would be helping one of his friends to move. Not just any friend mark you, but one of the same friends who failed to show up. We were taken aback; the natural human expectation was, "How can you be helping your friend who had failed to honor his commitment to you?" Then I said to my wife, our son is a better teacher than we are; in fact, he is teaching us. His behavioral standards are higher than ours; bad behavior is not his teacher.

Here it is; human nature says, "Get even," "do unto others as they have done unto you," but here he was teaching us or living out the lesson we teach our children that bad behavior or inferior standards should never be our teachers.

So, my wife and I were taken to school by our son. How about you? Are you allowing bad behavior or inferior standards of others to become your teachers?

A single thorn can prick a thousand hearts. (Saadi Shirazi)

39 Control freaks need not apply

The snowstorm on Tuesday, Jan 28, 2014, popularly called "Snowmageddon" brought a new sense of reality of how powerless we can be when we are accustomed to being in control of the events and outcomes in our daily lives. I know many of us were caught off-guard and joined the stampeding masses (think herd mentality) in leaving the offices early to attend to the safety of our families and loved ones as a result of this weather event. Much of what transpired in the next 12-18 hours was a test of our abilities to truly control and influence our outcomes.

Here is the struggle I faced, and I am sure many of you had the same. I normally have a 33-mile commute using the highway with an average commute time of 70 minutes. On that fateful Tuesday, I spent 3 hours trying to get to the last 4 miles to my home, watching cars dancing in an un-choreographed manner as they went skidding, kissing each other and spinning in wild delight. My young daughter works at a hospital on the top-end of I-285 (a 64 miles highway that runs around the perimeter of Atlanta). Knowing that she would have a challenge driving on the snowy/icy roads and the dangers present, we advised her to stay at a hotel. Well, being independent-minded, she decided to make the trip home starting out at 4:45 PM. She made her decision; I could not control that.

As she travelled along I-285, we were constantly on the phone, giving her tips and thinking of alternate routes to use. Since I was ahead of her and travelling the same route, I could see the dangers and hazards before she did and advised her to take alternative routes. Again, she decided to use the tried and proven route (being comfortable with what she knows). When I realized that the highway I was on was a menace, not wanting her to experience the same ordeal, I advised her to use another route. Well, again, she opted not to and eventually encountered stand-still traffic. I eventually made it home. We were monitoring the traffic conditions on television, and on the internet and feeding all this information to her via her cell phone.

My wife and I wanted to know how she was doing on gas; we thought of driving out to rescue her (I have a 4-wheel drive vehicle with anti-skid). She had half of a tank of gas. After she was in the same spot for 2 hours, I called 911, who told me that the county public workers were on their way with a salt truck. We kept in contact with her, trying to lift her spirits. One of the traffic updates stated that there was a 20-car pile-up, and the road was closed in both directions. My daughter then told us that she had 1 bar on the phone. We soon discovered that the cell phone was dead when she failed to respond to her text.

All the family was on alert; my wife was on pins, needles, tacks and nails. At that time, we both came to the same conclusion: we could not control the outcome of the situation; we were powerless and impotent. This was not ours to manage. We had tried to influence and control the outcome of the situation to no avail. We had to release our control, surrender, and repress our innate desire to be in command. We had to relax and refocus on preparing for her when she got home. Well, the good news is, 8 hours later, we heard the crunching of ice, and seeing her car, we were overjoyed and ecstatic. She was home and safe. Looking back, we now know that we can provide input in the hope that we can shape and influence outcomes, but we must know when to resign, release, and relinquish control.

So, as we look back, do you find yourself holding on to things for too long, not knowing when to let go? Do you find yourself in a constant state of "flux" and anxiety trying to control the outcome of events? Do you know how to relax and accept the changes in life? Do you know when to release and re-focus your energies and efforts on other objectives that are more beneficial? Do you know when enough is enough?

When the pain of holding on is greater than the pain of letting go, we will let go.

40 Wearing another person's skin

I heard this story recently and thought how true this is in other facets of life.

A gorilla, having recently given birth at a zoo for unknown reasons, rejected her offspring. The zookeepers were amazed at this. How could a mother reject her own? It goes against the laws of nature. So, the attendants knew they had to act. When they approached the baby gorilla, it shied away. Somehow, it recognized these creatures as foreigners. So, the savvy zookeepers donned a gorilla suit and retrieved the baby gorilla. They were then able to calm its fears and feed it, all the time mimicking the behavior of a mother gorilla.

So, very often, we find ourselves in situations where we are unable to make progress. One party holds its ground, not willing to change, and the other does the same. But if we " we can better empathize and relate to them. In fact, such behavioral changes in making accommodations for others who have different perspectives, experiences, and viewpoints will only foster and enhance greater harmony.

What does it look like to wear the skin of another person?

1. Take the time to actively listen to their story and be patient, with a desire to learn and understand.
2. Try to see things from their perspective and their viewpoints.
3. Ask questions that can better allow you to relate to their experiences.
4. Try not to pre-judge the person or make assumptions.
5. Demonstrate empathy; let them know you care.

So, are you willing to wear someone else's skin to better understand and relate to them?

I thought all other men were animals until I realized I was one of them.

41 Shipwrecked wishes and opportunities

Most of us look back on life and shake our heads in disgust when we realize that we had the power and the opportunity at hand to make a significant difference in our lives for the better and failed to make the most of it. Here is a story that brings this to the fore.

Three men were shipwrecked on a remote island. They had spent several weeks on the island, slowly accepting their fate that they may never get off. Well, as most stories go, one particular day, one of them noticed a bottle that had washed up on the beach. One thought it contained a message, and then quickly another said, “That could be a magic bottle.” “How can you tell?” said another. “Well, there is only one way to know; let's rub the bottle." Sure enough, they rubbed the bottle and, to their amazement, out popped a genie. He then demanded, "Why have you disturbed me? You each have one wish, so use it wisely." The men could not believe it, here was their opportunity to get off the island. The genie asked the first man what his wish was. The man did not take long to come up with an answer, "I wish to be back on Wall St. in my office." Before he could finish uttering the last word, he was in his office. The genie asked the second man, "And what is your wish?" The man quickly responded that he missed his family so much; his wish was to be with them. Whoosh, he was back with his family. Then, the genie turned to the third man and told him to make his wish. The man thought long and hard and then said, "This is very hard for me; my friends and I were very close, and we consulted each other before we made our decisions. Man, this is hard." Thinking aloud, he said, "I only wish my friends were here to help me come up with my wish."

Well, there you have it. How often do we find ourselves with opportunities that can advance our cause and yet we blow it? And worse yet, we sometimes negatively impact others. So, what are you doing with the opportunities that are presented to you? Do you blow them and then regret the decisions later? Do you consider the long-term outcome before you act?

Hindsight is foresight painfully too late; the hour hand of the clock never seems to move while you are watching it.

42 Jumping from the frying the pan into the fire

Most of us are driven by certain passions and motivations to satisfy some intrinsic needs or desires. Occasionally, we find ourselves in situations which at times may become unbearable or as they say in the Caribbean, "too hot". We believe that the situation is so overwhelming that the first chance that presents itself causes us to head for "cooler climes". But not all that glitters is gold.

We often think that the grass is greener on the other side, only to realize after we make a move that what looked verdant and appealing from afar was nothing more than green weeds. Too late we discover we cannot undo the commitments to go back to our prior situation or state. This is why I say it is better to stay in the frying pan than jump into the fire. At least when one is in the frying pan, there is some insulation or substance between you and the fire. Not so when we are in the fire; there is no barrier, and the flames are in direct contact with us.

So, when you are next tempted to make that move because the heat is too much, do check that if you jump, your leap is long enough to land you outside of the flames. In short, "Look before you leap."

Somethings to consider before you make the leap: ask yourself these questions.

1. How well-equipped am I to handle the situation?
2. Do I know all the facts about the situation before making the leap?
3. What are the pitfalls?
4. How will I be treated?
5. Will the change fit into my long-term goals and objectives?
6. Do I know anyone who is currently in that situation I can talk with?

It is a foolish person who signs a contract and then asks questions after the fact. – ***(The Bible)***.

43 Two objects cannot occupy the same space at the same time

One lesson I learned the hard way in learning to drive was that "no two objects can occupy the same space at the same time." (And no, I did not have any accidents while learning to drive). When teaching my children to drive, I instilled in them that simple rule. So much so that whenever we went out and saw an accident, they would proclaim, "I guess they did not know about the rule; no two objects can occupy the same space at the same time." So, as human beings, we end up surprisingly trying to do the exact same thing, trying to occupy the same space at the same time, physically, mentally, and emotionally.

Unfortunately, these incidents, or rather the outcome, if not controlled or tempered, can escalate very quickly into conflicts, fights, and quarrels. As in an auto accident, one party is usually right and the other "wrong," as well as both parties being "at fault." The collision of individuals is bad enough. What is even worse is when we resort to our "rights," using pride, position, power, and authority to drive the outcome in our favor.

We resent having to surrender our rights, especially if we know the other person is wrong. We hold our high ground and expect the other person to yield, to ask forgiveness, to beg for mercy, to admit wrongdoing before we budge. We resort to verbal altercations to "keep our space." We seek reinforcements from those sympathetic to our cause to defend our position and dig in. But what if we took the unusual path of surrendering our rights? What if we took the wrongdoing? What if we gave up our "space" to the other person? What if we initiated the peace even when we have the right to be right?

Sometimes, it is better to yield our rights rather than having our rights read to us or our rites read over us.

44 Habits and routines can become our undoing

Several years ago, I discovered the importance of communication precision or rather, the lack thereof. We all have behavioral patterns and routines, things we do repeatedly day in and day out without giving much thought to how they are done, allowing us to be successful in our everyday activities. These standard "processes" help us to optimize our activities and prevent chaos and confusion. None of us like it when our routines are interrupted, disturbed, or disrupted without our say-so.

I had the unfortunate experience of seeing firsthand what it means to have your routine disrupted. Taking out the garbage is a pretty mundane event and really calls for very little effort. As in most households, I (the husband and father) was responsible for getting the garbage into the bin and then rolling it out to the curbside to be picked up by the garbage collectors. On one fateful night, I got home late from some event and, as usual, got ready to pull the garbage bin to the curb when I noticed several large white garbage bags sitting in the garage. Without giving this any thought, I threw the bags into the garbage bin and rolled them to the curb, knowing the garbage truck normally comes early in the morning. Great, the husband does his duty. Happy wife, happy life!

Well, the following day, I got a rude awakening. I received a phone call from my wife asking me if I had taken the clothes to the cleaners. I told her no; she normally takes the clothes to the cleaners. Well, she enquired about the bags she had left out as she was not able to find them. I said, "You mean the garbage bags that were in the garage?" She, of course, said yes; she had placed them there temporarily with the intent of putting them in the car to take to the cleaners later. Well, you can imagine what transpired when we both discovered I had disposed of her perfectly good clothes. Needless to say, we realized that we both had erred; she in putting the clothes in regular garbage bags (not the regular dry-cleaning laundry bag), leaving them in a place where they could readily be mistaken for trash and me for not checking why I had extra garbage.

So, the question to be answered is, are we aware of our impact on the routine of others? Do we know when we have disrupted their routines? Are we prepared to deal with the fallout and the consequences? Many will say, "Accidents do happen." But the bigger question is, "What did I do to cause the accident?" Are we so lost in our routines and behavioral patterns, taking things for granted without questioning anything that may be out of the ordinary? Do we take the time to assess what impact we may have on the behavioral norms of others based on our actions?

Time can only be measured when there is a change or movement of some kind.

45 As a person thinks, so is he

Life can be such an amazing paradox and parody at times. We all enter this world with just about the same mental quotient or, rather, what I would call the "thought quotient." That is, we were all given a mind to use as we choose. So how is it that we can have different people who start life on the same level playing field but go through life totally differently? Some may say that is not a true statement, but think about it for a moment, we all came into this world with the same ability to think and shape who we are by what and how we think of ourselves. Our thoughts shape us in becoming who and what we are. We become what we think. Every action we take starts with a thought: to move, to sit, to eat, to run, to talk, to re-act, to imagine, to hope, to despair, to choose, to go, to stay, to complain, to commend, to work, to stop. (I do concede there are some basal, reflexive actions that require no thought).

Our actions, behaviors, attitudes, dispositions, and the people we ultimately become are the sum total of our thoughts. We can choose to worry and become anxious and fearful. We can choose to think positively and become people of courage, action, and hope. Our thoughts shape our outlook on life, not just our experiences. What we think about our experiences and how we imagine life to be from a mental state ultimately shapes who we are and how we engage in life from that point on.

We are not defined by our experiences, places of birth, residence, social status, culture, or education but rather by how we think. Two people can have the same experience but end up having different perspectives. Two people can see a glass with water, one sees it as partially empty and the other as partially full. Our thoughts allow us to see ourselves as victors or victims, conquerors or losers, optimists or pessimists, realists or idealists.

When we begin to master our thought life and direct it to positive states, we start to become masters of who we are. No longer are we defined by what others think of us but rather by what we think of ourselves. We own who we are. We hold the handle of the knife, not the blade. So, next time you start thinking that life is unfair, re-examine the germ of that thought and shape it to how you can take advantage of the unevenness of life's playing field.

He who holds the handle of the knife, cuts the cake.

46 Unmet expectations can cause a foul odor

I recently ran into a former high school classmate of mine. I could not help but notice this large garbage bag he was carrying, slung over his shoulders. As I approached him, I had to force every muscle in my being not to turn and get away from him as fast as I could due to the awful stench that was emanating from him. But I was extremely curious as to the reason he was carrying such a large garbage bag and, more importantly, wanted to know how life had treated him after all these years. So, without being too conspicuous, I tried holding my breath as we caught up. In our final year in high school, he was voted as the person most likely to succeed. He had won a scholarship to some elite university and was well on his way. He had also married. Life we thought could not have been better for him. So, you can understand my curiosity in wanting to know how he ended up in this state.

I soon realized that the stench was coming from the garbage bag he was carrying. We quickly got re-acquainted, and I soon found out that life had floored him, or rather, his response to life had him floored. He was extremely cynical and scathing in his outlook on life and in a sense, towards me. He shared how he graduated magna cum laude from his college and got a prestigious job on Wall Street. The expectations he had set for himself were that in ten years or less, he would make a partner in the firm. The first shock he received was when he was passed over for that sought-after promotion that he knew he well deserved, more so than the guys who got it. He had paid his dues and was lavishly praised for his accomplishments, but the promotion was not forthcoming. He had married what he thought was the "love of his life" and thought they were on their way to heaven when he had a bad accident that left him almost crippled. His wife stayed with him during the early weeks of his ordeal, but when the doctors told him that he would never fully recover, she eventually left him, saying she had no expectations of remaining married to an "invalid." He soon discovered that the company he had worked for at the time of the accident failed to even support him once his insurance ran out. The only things he received were flowers in the hospital and "nice" get-well cards. When he contacted them to return to work, they told him to take his time to heal.

He eventually had to live with his cousin; all his savings were wiped out by the hospital bills that the insurance could not cover. He had become desolate. He refused to forgive life for what happened to him and cherished every painful thought. His story was that of a man whose expectations in life were not met. He expected his company to be there for him; he expected his wife to be there for him, he expected to make it big with his company, he expected that he would be wealthy; he expected that he could do what he wanted with life. So, as one expectation after another failed to materialize, he first became disappointed, then sad, and then frustrated. He decided that he would keep these unmet expectations and the resultant "pain" in a bag. This was the bag that I saw him with. Over the years, he has filled the bag with bitterness, resentment, anger, and cynicism, which only got bigger and bigger with each new episode of unfulfilled expectation. The foul odor emanating from the bag was from years of bitterness, resentment, frustration, anger, disappointment, and anguish resulting from the unrealized expectations he had held on to.

So, what about you? How big is your bag? What is in your bag? How do you handle situations when your expectations, whether real or unrealistic, are not realized? What do you do with the disappointments and sadness that often are the fruit of such unmet expectations? Have you become so scented with the fragrance of unfulfilled expectations that you no longer know what it means to be fresh?

Hope deferred makes the heart sick*. – *(The Bible).

47 Which side has the truth?

Growing up as kids, we enjoyed being asked: "witty" questions that would challenge our intellect or "smarts." One question was: which side of the chicken has the most feathers? The common answer usually given was the "side with the tail. Then, we were told that those answers were wrong; the outside of the chicken had the most feathers. This witty childhood quiz is just a precursor to how we process and make judgments based on information presented to us. Very often we find ourselves being asked to make judgments on issues or situations related to people. A person or friend shares with us an experience or incident in which they would like us to provide some judgment to help them; let's say this is a disagreement or conflict with another person.

How do we assess the situation? How objective are we in our assessment of the information presented? Do we seek to get additional information to make a reasonable or objective decision? Do we attempt to get information from the other person's perspective? What roles do our biases, prejudices, or idiosyncrasies play in how we decide? Are we able to remove our emotions from the assessment of the situation?

If we use our "factory default setting" in processing, then we may very well find ourselves telling them that the tail of the chicken has the most feathers. We must be careful not to give answers that people want to hear but present the truth in such a way that they can see it for what it is and come to their own conclusions or decisions. Another question: how many sides does a nickel have?

As my mother said, there are always three sides to every story: your side, my side, and the truth.

48 Second opinion matters

At some time or another, we have all been faced with a predicament that causes us to seek out advice from others. More often than not, we sometimes tend to act on the first piece of advice given, especially those from experts in the field. But what if there are other alternatives to be explored that can yield the same or better results with lower cost or less time? Here is a story I heard recently that drives home this point.

A man had trouble sleeping at night, a situation that had plagued him since childhood. He always felt that there was a "boogey" man under his bed. Here he was as an adult, still having the same fears at night. So, in desperation, he consulted a psychiatrist who, after hearing his plight, told him he could have him cured in 12 weeks. The therapy would entail 1-hour weekly sessions of $200 per week for 12 weeks for a total of $2,400. Well, the man on hearing that, said he would think it over.

A few weeks later, the man had a chance run-in with the psychiatrist, who wanted to know why he had never followed through on his recommendation. The man responded he had been cured of his fears. The good doctor asked how so? The man explained that he was telling his barber about his condition, who suggested that all he needed to do was to cut off the legs from the bed. For a $20 haircut, he took the barber's advice, went home, and cut the legs off his bed. He has been sleeping like a "baby" since then.

Not discounting the advice of the professionals, it is always good to get input from others. Very often, the solution to our problems is closer than we think. I keep a good dose of older, intimate friends whose wisdom I can readily tap into. What about you? Who do you consult when you have decisions to make? Are you seeking other alternative options or are you going along with the first piece of advice given?

***When you come to a fork in the road, find out where it leads before you take it*.**

49 Tongue-prints, it's not your story to tell

My wife has a saying that she repeatedly shares at home and in professional group settings, "It is not your story to tell." That is, we do not have the right to share unless the person has given it to us. We do not broadcast another person's personal situation to others without their permission. From time to time, we receive information that, based on its "perceived importance," we would readily like to share with others. Sometimes, this may indeed fall in the line of just plain gossiping or rumormongering.

As we go about deciding to share information with others, it is wise to ask and answer these questions before putting the tongue into drive:

1) Do I have the right to share this information?

2) What value will the sharing of this information serve to my audience?

3) What harm can be done by sharing this information if it is about others?

4) Am I breaching any confidentiality or trust in sharing the information?

5) Would I be willing to share this information if the other person was present?

The tongue, like our fingers, has its own unique print. What does your tongue-print look like?

By your tongue, you are known.

50 Helping others get to the next level

All of us are at different levels of maturity, competency, and satisfaction in life. We all have opportunities before us that will warrant trying to get to the next level. More often than not, getting to that next level may require assistance from others who are already at that level.

I was in a discussion recently with a couple on that topic. The wife stated that her husband was at a higher level of managing his emotions in the relationship. I then asked the husband, if that is the case, how does he help his wife get to a higher level? His response was a little surprising. I really had expected him to say something like, "Well, I would pull her up to my level"; instead, he said, "I go down to her level and then help her up." Mmmmm, I thought. For him, even though he was at a higher level, he did not use this as a position of power but rather donned the garment of humility to come alongside his wife to help her up the ladder.

So, how do we go about helping others to get to the next level?

Do we get in the hole with them to push them up, or do we extend a hand down to pull them up? What if our hands are too short to reach them? What if there is too much gap between the levels? What if the person is much heavier than we are and will pull us down?

A person should not be congratulated on the heights he has reached but rather from the depths he has risen. – (Frederick Douglas).

51 Wanting versus doing

One of the beauties of cross-cultural experience is seeing how we behave as a group based on common societal habits versus other cultures. Take the case of expressing appreciation to others. Very often, the message goes like this, whether verbally or in written form. "I want to thank you for.... I want to say thanks for ...", "I would like to say thanks to.... Let's break this apart. "I want" or "I would like to" is a future state.

The statement says that a person has a desire to express thanks to do something in the future. How about just saying thanks rather than wanting to? Think about this. I want to go on vacation to Costa Rica, is different from I am going on vacation to Costa Rica. I listened to President Obama once expressing thanks to the military for the war efforts in Afghanistan, and he did not say, "I want to thank…" he went straight ahead and said, "I thank the men and women of our military for their service."

So many of us have incorporated this phrase into our communication style, and it has become second nature. Take the time to first test yourself if you are guilty of this line and pattern of communication. So, how do we break the pattern? Let's carefully think about what we want to accomplish, execute or take action on. Then, just speak to it. Intentionally break the cycle with conscious focus and effort. Correct yourself every time you default to this line. Listen for this when others speak and mentally make the correction.

A want is a desire; it is yet to be attained, so we need to just get pass this and "just do it" like NIKE. Can you see the power behind the slogan and how it is action-oriented? No beating around the bush. Just do it, period. But of course, all of this is for naught as we understand the intent due to our cultural norms and acceptance.

I want to thank you for reading this; as soon as I get around to it, I would like to thank you.

52 Gone fishing

My son has found a new passion in fishing and belatedly is discovering that it is far more demanding than he first thought. His initial action was just to buy a line, bait it, and throw the line in the water, hoping for the fish to bite. Well, he soon realized this was an effort in futility. For several days, he caught nothing. He even started fishing in other ponds, but he only caught frustration, dead branches, and garbage. He started consulting more experienced fishermen, researching on the internet and discovered that fishing was not an art but rather a science. The time-of-day matters, the temperature matters, the bait, and the type of fish to be caught all mattered. Knowing the types of fish in the water and the food they eat, how they hunt for the food, and the preferred location where the fish tend to wait or hunt for their food were all part of the ingredients for success. The techniques used to stimulate the fish to bite on his bait were very important. After getting some instructions on how to fish for specific fish with another fisherman showing him the ropes, he started catching fish and big ones, too. (This is no fish story).

So, he could share with me some key life lessons he had learned. If you want to accomplish something, invest in the tools and methods for attaining it. Expect to experience disappointments and setbacks and consult others who have walked the path. Take the risk of doing it; not trying is not an option for success.

Life for all of us is about fishing. What kind of fish are we going after, or are we hoping any fish will do? Do we have the right tools to take it on? Do we surround ourselves with coaches and cheerleaders? Are we willing to take the risks? Are we prepared to groom our patience and learn from our mistakes? How tenacious and resilient are we when setbacks occur? Are we bold enough to fish in other ponds?

Give a man a fish; he feeds his family for a day - he becomes dependent on a handout! Teach a man to fish; he feeds his family for a season - he depletes the fish stock. Teach a man to reproduce fish; he feeds his family for generations - he only has to worry about pollution.

53 It's not my paint - culpability and taking ownership

Several years ago, we contracted with a painter to paint the interior of our house. In some places, we were changing the color. Upon completion of the job, we discovered that there were paint smudges on some of the trims, ceilings, and borders. When we brought this to the attention of the painter, his response was, "That was not my paint." That was his standard response, even in cases where the smudge was the same color as the paint just used. So, we shared this with the family, and we have noticed that when someone fails to take ownership of a "miss" or something they did that they do not want to own up to or correct, we say, "It's not my paint."

So how about you? Do you find yourself shying away from actions that you should have taken to address a situation? Do you find yourself stepping over an obstacle in the path, saying, "I did not put it there?" Do you readily take ownership of things when they turn out wrong, and you contribute to the outcome? Do you hide behind excuses?

Part of being culpable says that we take ownership and are held accountable for our actions. It also says that when we see something amiss, we will do whatever is necessary to help correct that situation. There are two acts of culpability- 1: the act of commission - taking ownership and full accountability for our actions. 2: the act of omission - failure to take ownership of our actions or turning a blind eye to things that we have the power and authority to address.

Excuses are tools for non-achievers.

54 Darkness, blindness and light

When a person is blind and lives in the darkness, moving him into the light will not cause him to see. He will only see when his blindness is removed. We tend to forget this principle, especially when we are trying to get others to see our point of view. They have lived for a long time in their world, seeing things only from their perspective, and then somehow, when we move them into our world with their blindness (still seeing things from their perspective), we expect them to readily appreciate and understand our point of view or see things the way we do.

We expend enormous amounts of energy, time, and effort trying to convince, persuade, and influence the other person to see things the way we do, all to no avail.

What could be wrong? We erroneously believe that if we can get a person into the light of our world, they will see things the way we do. Wrong! They can only see things the way we do when their mental/emotional blindness is gone.

Yes, let's be real. It makes no sense to try to talk to someone to see your point of view when they are blinded by their biases, idiosyncrasies and dispositions. Very often, our futile attempt to get them to see the "light" from our perspective leaves us and them sometimes frustrated. The longer you persist with no change, the more often it can lead to anger, bitterness and resentment towards the person. We call them names such as pig-headed, stubborn, obstinate, and head stuck in the sand. You get the point.

So, next time you find yourself trying to get a person to see things from your perspective, do ask the question: are they still blind, or are you expecting them to see because you have tried to enlighten them?

A blind person cannot see the colors until their eyes are open.

55 Cross-wired behavior

We recently had our heating and air conditioning unit replaced. As you can imagine, this was not an inexpensive operation, and fortunately, the unit failed during the fall. However, during the winter, we noticed that the rooms were extremely cold, so we notified the company (who will remain nameless for now) who did the work of this. Of course, they thought that an adjustment of the thermostat would easily remediate the situation. Well, that did not resolve the problem. So, they ended up opening the unit and checking the electrical wiring. Only then did they discover that the unit was wired incorrectly. The wires used to turn on the cold air were wired to the heater and vice versa. So here we were in the middle of winter, and the unit, even though it had the right temperature setting on the thermostat, was only blowing cold air.

So many of us are like that; we are hard-wired, and our behavior betrays who we are. Changing the room temperature setting in our lives does not cause us to behave differently. Our hardwiring is tied to our beliefs, values, perceptions, and identity. Until we change the internal wiring, we will always produce the same outcome.

So how about you? Do you know if your wiring is connected to the right circuit? Do you find yourself getting easily angered or irritated when things do not go your way? Do you make light of situations that warrant serious consideration? Do you blow hot air when cool air is what is needed?

How do you change your hard wiring?

1. Try new things, learn new things.

2. Meet and engage with others who are different from you.

3. Undo a bad habit with intentional and repeated practice.

We cultivate the things that we celebrate – (Buddy Hoffman).

56 Change requires time for adjusting

I was at a family event some time ago, where the hostess had gone to extensive effort to prepare a wonderful lasagna dish from scratch. However, as she was getting ready to set up, she placed the cooled "Pyrex" dish containing the lasagna on the stove surface, not realizing it was still very hot. A few minutes later, we heard a loud popping sound and noticed that the "Pyrex" dish was cracked all over. Unknowingly, she had placed the "Pyrex" dish on the hot stove surface, forgetting that it was extremely hot.

Change is a way of life unless, of course, one is dead, and even then, change still occurs. We are surrounded by an almost infinite set of variables that constantly introduce changes to our environment, lifestyles, and expectations. Change, then, is to be expected. However, quite often, we find ourselves struggling to accept the change, especially where the impact may result in an unpleasant change of our "comfortability," security, or that which we have become accustomed to. When a change is being introduced, especially one in which we have had no input, it is important to allow time for transition. This transition allows us to absorb and digest the change, to ask questions, and to work it out.

The more significant the change, the more time is needed to absorb, digest, adjust, and acclimatize. Failure to provide this period of transition can cause us to become anxious, stressed, angry, and hostile, especially if the change is not one we readily want. So, the next time you go through a change, do ensure that you allow yourself some time to adjust and transition to the change.

If you cannot change the direction of the wind, change the direction of your sails.

57 Tied to the stake

I remember, as a child, going to the circus and then, as an adult, doing the same with my family. One of the more entertaining events was the acts involving the elephants. How was it possible that these powerful animals allowed themselves to be mastered and maneuvered by their trainers? Since then, I have discovered that this is based on the process used in their training. The trainers start out with infant elephants and keep them chained to a stake. The elephant, over time, knows he cannot extend beyond the limits and boundaries of the chain. So, as he becomes older and the chain is removed, he continues to believe that he is attached to the chain and will not venture out of his invisible limits.

Now, as human beings, we sometimes behave in the same way as these grown elephants. We find ourselves artificially chained to the effects of our past mistakes. We become trapped, stifled and limit our potential to advance because we subconsciously are tied to our past mistakes or rather the negative impact of them.

So, as you continue on the journey of life, do check to see if you are bound or are still chained to the mistakes of your earlier life. Do you find that fear as a result of past failures keeps you from taking a risk? How about just taking a small risk to undo the chain? If fear from a prior mistake is holding you captive, then how about partnering with someone to take on the challenge in order to break the chain? Celebrate your advance and success, and keep at it.

What is preventing you from breaking from that self-imposed chain to become a better you?

Our past should not be a cemetery but a garden from which we can grow a better version of ourselves.

58 We are the by-product of the company we keep

I am always amazed to see news stories of some person who got involved in some illegal activity, with parents and other family members bemoaning the fact that this is a "good" kid who got caught up in bad company. He is not to be blamed for his actions; this was a one-time event, and the blame lies squarely with the other persons involved.

So, as you think about this, we must ask the question: what role do we play in choosing the friends we make? Do we gravitate to people who can lift us up or those who have negative influences? Do we select friends based on their character and integrity? What does their track record look like? Is this a person I want to have protecting my back in a fight? What desirable character traits does this person have?

Is the person caustic, abrasive, rude, vulgar or mean? Do they respect you for who you are? Are they reliable and trustworthy? Is this the person you would want your child to bring home as a friend?

None of us are under pressure to select the types of friends we end up with. Very often, we select friends who share the same values and beliefs. We feel accepted and validated by our choice of friends. Over time, the influence our friends have on us starts to leave its mark on us. As my grandmother would say, "Show me the friends you keep, and I will show you the measure of a person you are." How about you? What do your friends say about the type of person you are?

Bad company corrupts good manners, birds of a feather flock together.

59 Language is more than words

My daughter was doing some homework recently and shared with me the fact that we only remember less than 10% of what is said but tend to remember 70-90% of how the information is delivered. By "how," I mean the body language that accompanied the communication or the information was delivered with, along with the vocal tone. Effective communicators exploit this technique and use the "how" to get their message across. Think of comedians, actors, and musicians; they wrap the information they present in strong body language. Notice that the music is now wrapped with videos to better convey the message. They intend to leave a lasting impression on their audiences. (If given a choice, most of us would rather watch a movie about the subject rather than just reading the book. Our memories encounter greater stimulation when not just intellectual content is conveyed but visual and colorful renderings of the subject matter.)

Think of your own experiences and see if you are more apt to remember "how" you felt when something was communicated more so than "what" was communicated. I was at a recent event, and the speaker was choked with tears as the message was being delivered. Surprise, surprise, most people after the event remarked more about the emotional visuals of the presenter rather than what was said.

So, next time you deliver a message or are attempting to get a point across consider how you may use your body (hand gesticulations, facial expressions, body movements, etc.) and vocal tone to reinforce that message. At the same time, consider how using your body language inappropriately can negate your message or detract from what you want to convey. Working with younger children, I have discovered much of the pain of interpersonal rivalry results from body language, not just the spoken language.

Do you find yourself laughing at someone else's predicament? Do you speak with your nerves? Do you readily find that your emotions (good or bad) dominate the conversation and stifle the message? Then, step back and ask yourself if this is the way you want to communicate. Am I distorting the message with my body language, or should I be more intentional in my body language to be a more effective communicator? I only hope I was effective in getting my point across to you, minus the body language.

My body speaks louder than my words, but it is a horrible speller.

60 Asking questions after the fact

It is a foolish thing to ask questions after you have signed a contract. We all like to believe that we are wise and sensible individuals or, as we say, where I am from, "city-smart or street-smart"; however, there are times we tend to do things that question that grain of wisdom. I was recently at an event where a person discovered after signing a contract for some work to be done on his home that he was liable for some significant expenses. How could this have happened to him? Well, it was all in the fine print on the back side of the contract that he failed to pay adequate attention to.

So, you say, that would not happen to me. I am too "street smart" for that. But as you rent a car, do you read all the fine print before you sign on the dotted line when all you want is to get on with your business? When you open a bank account do you take the time to consult with your lawyers to better understand the fine print? And for crying out loud, for those of us who have ever had to purchase real estate, car, or sign for a loan, do we really understand all that is written on a multiplicity of documents tendered for our signatures?

Think about this: those who are on the other side of the contract have had their lawyers do all the leg work, they have had time to adequately shape the contract to their liking, and more importantly, to put most, if not all, the burden and liability on you. So, as much as it lies within you, always try to get your questions raised and answered before you sign on the dotted line. (Yes, and do not fall for the time-sensitive options; if you do not sign now, you will miss out on this once-in-a-lifetime opportunity).

Most people become smarter not so much from their successes but rather from their failures.

61 Eating half-baked cake

I enjoy watching historical movies, and I was humored by an adaptation of Joan of Arc where, in one scene, the king is asking Joan to commit her soldiers to the battle before they have completed building the army and raising the supplies needed. Her response was, "Do you eat your cake before it is fully baked?"

In so many ways, we are so much like that king or have allowed ourselves to become like him. Very often; we find ourselves in a mad rush to get things done without thinking about the final price we ultimately pay for this speed, quite often sacrificing quality for expediency. Our society has glorified instant gratification as the new "normal"; patience is fast becoming a lost virtue. Notice that even in the restaurant business, we now have a category called "fast food." The need for speed is driving much of what we do. All around us is the cry rather than the wailing of "get it done faster."

Companies are being pressured to get their products to the market faster and faster. Big businesses, especially those in retail are pushing the envelope to get products to their customers faster than ever before. Yes, we want it and want it now! The credit card industry has shown us how we can have it all now and pay later; electronic gadgets are taking us captives or, more aptly, making us slaves. Yes, these devices have enabled us to be more productive and stay better connected, but they have fueled our appetite for instancy.

Once, you would only upgrade your mobile phones every two years; now, some companies have introduced programs to constantly get the latest model within the year. We are not willing to wait anymore. We drive and text. We walk around like zombies glued to our mobile devices, forgetting the social graces of just saying, "Hello; how are you today? Or have a nice day." We are even trying to sleep faster and with fewer hours. As a society, we have become more technologically advanced, which in turn has only contributed to increased stress in our lives. Hyper-tension and related heart diseases continue to be the crowning champions of our mad dash to the finish line. In a sense, we all want to be the next Usain Bolt to run our "dash" in record time, not knowing the price to be ultimately paid. So, the next time you are about to eat your cake, ask yourself, "is it fully baked?" And do allow some time for it to cool before eating it.

What will your dash read when you have reached the finish line of life?

62 A piece of peace

As children growing up it was inculcated in us to strive for peace. We should always seek a peaceful outcome for any situation that we are in, even if it means sacrificing our rights. Many of us struggle with that. Intrinsic in our behavior is to come out of a situation feeling that our position is justified, and we were right; peace is secondary.

Well sometime back, I got a new lesson in how to pursue peace, the peace that requires courage, stamina, and effort to achieve. Not the one where you can easily walk away and hope that things will remain calm. No, I am talking about the one where you must go to the next level of discussion, striving for justice. My wife, as always, had booked our vacation accommodation well in advance of the event to house two families with a total of 8 people. The other family would be joining us later. When we arrived at the resort, we discovered that the rooms provided were on the third floor with no elevator access, and some of the amenities and features she had requested were missing. We struggled with the luggage up the stairs, and I personally thought the rooms were worth it. Wonderful view! Great!

Well, my wife was not wooed or wowed by the elegance of the rooms or their furnishings. She wanted a room on the ground floor or one with elevator access. The resort management apologized profusely, saying that they had no more rooms available and that we would just have to live with what we had. Now, there and then, I thought and said this to her for "peace's sake." Let's just enjoy what we have, highlighting all the finer points of the facility. No, she insisted that she specifically asked for a ground-floor unit. She then told me that there was such a thing as righteous peace. I said, "What?" She then went to show us what this looked like. She called the hotel management very calmly and controlled and went up the management chain, making her case with the precision of an expert lawyer.

The outcome was that she was able to get the rooms on the ground floor as she had requested when she made the booking. That was a lesson in righteous peace. We need to know when to walk away from a situation and let matters be and when not to settle. Peace is not just the absence of strife but rather the pursuit of that which is right, allowing others to live peacefully.

So how about you? Do you know when to just live for "peace's sake" or when to pursue "righteous peace"? Do you know the difference between battle and war, when to fight and when to let go?

Righteousness is the bed on which peace sleeps.

63 Fitting square pegs into round holes

Ever so often, we are confronted with situations that can best be described as trying to fit a "square peg into a round hole" or a "round peg into a square hole". Whatever the circumstance, the challenge we face is how to make the most of the situation and the conditions that seem to be in conflict or a mismatch with what we desire or hope for. Sometimes, we represent that "square peg," defined by our values, expectations, positions, and feelings that somehow, we cannot get to match up with the situation at hand represented by the "round hole." We end up in dissonance and have a hard time adjusting to the situation. What should one do? How do you fit a square peg into a round hole? One immediate option is to pound the peg into the hole. Well, that will only cause a lot of pain, grief, and agony for both the peg and the hole, especially if people are involved. (We have all seen that ad with the mechanics as boys; "hit it, Johnny, hit it, it will go in," and then as adults doing the same thing). Then, it becomes a huge challenge when it is time to extricate the peg from the hole; it is now solidly wedged into place.

Yet another option is to widen the hole, that seems to be a feasible solution, but again, we may not have the resources, power, authority, or time to widen the hole (that is, change the situation) to accommodate the peg. This approach will leave us just as frustrated as trying to hammer the peg into the hole in option 1. Conversely make the peg smaller so that it can fit into the hole without any permanent damage. We tend to have far more control, authority, and power over ourselves (the peg) to make the necessary adjustments to fit into the hole. How do you make the peg smaller? We can strive for a compromise instead of demanding that our position must be met and be satisfied, we can yield or surrender some of our rights and privileges, we can concede and move on, and we can take a time out. The fact is we have the ability to change the shape and size of the peg more so than the hole.

So, next time you are confronted with a square peg and a round hole, ask yourself, "do I really need to get into that hole?" As for the peg, what adjustments can I make to fit into that hole if the hole is something very important to me? Or better yet, do I even need to get the peg into the hole?

I have learnt that by being flexible, I will never be bent out of shape.

64 Differences are what make us unique.

Some friends of mine recently recounted an experience they had with their 7-year-old granddaughter. While at the pool on vacation, she tried lifting off her bathing suit top, for which she received a stern rebuke from her parents that "girls are not to do that." Well later, they were given a tour of a military training facility, and the tour guide was highlighting the fact that both men and women do the same training, and there is nothing that a man can do that a woman cannot. The little girl then said, "That is not true." The tour guide insisted that this was indeed true, anything the guys can do, the girls can do. The little girl then curtly said, "Girls cannot take off their tops in public." So, there you have it.

We all like to know that we are different and are accepted for our differences and our uniqueness. But how often do you find yourself in situations where those differences are discounted? (I am not talking about being rude, disrespectful, or unkind, which is unbecoming behavior in any form).

In the workplace, we are told that our differences allow for different perspectives, but then we are challenged to fall in line with the status quo or the group mode; we get calibrated against 'the model" employees. We pride ourselves on being receptive to people who are different than us but then exclude them from our inner circles when they are not like us. We say we embrace each person's uniqueness, individuality, and abilities but then compare them to others. How often as a child did you hear the expression, "Why can't you be like so and so? How about you? Do you allow another person's differences to add value to the relationship, or do you wish them to be more like you?"

The only difference between you and me is that I am me, and you are you.

Without differences, there can be no identification.

65 Treasure hunting

Many of us pride ourselves in the fact that we can multi-task (doing several things at the same time) and not just merely doing them but doing them well. We believe that we are super-humans and can force our brains to concentrate on multiple cognitive activities concurrently and not compromise the efficacy of any of them.

I was recently watching a documentary on the subject, and there was one man in particular who thought he was the "king" of multitasking. He volunteered for an experiment with a university professor who was researching the topic. He was subsequently placed in a simulation lab and asked to do some of the normal everyday tasks that he claimed he had mastered as part of his multi-tasking exercise. Well, the results were very revealing. On the surface, he appeared to be doing multiple tasks concurrently, driving a car and steering through an obstacle course, talking on the phone, and reading some articles on his mobile device, but actually, he was not multitasking. The research demonstrated he had to briefly stop one activity to concentrate on the other, even though he was doing this in small bits of time. His activities were being done sequentially, albeit in small, repeated time segments; his brain, like 99% of the population, can only concentrate on one thing at a time. At no time whatsoever was it seen that his brain was processing multiple concurrent activities.

We foolishly think that we, too, can multi-task and not compromise the integrity of our actions or the outcome of our actions. My daily commute has allowed me to see first-hand some of the negative impacts of our vain attempts at multi-tasking. I am no longer surprised at the number of accidents I see because a person was driving and attempting to do something else (applying make-up, changing a radio set, putting down a cup, talking on the phone, reading billboards, reading a book, gazing at accidents etc.) at the same time.

Our brains can only focus on one thing at a time, and that point of interest or center of attention will always take precedence over the other things. So, how about you? Are you fooling yourself into believing that you can truly multi-task? Do you believe the fallacy that by attempting to do many things at the same time, you are being efficient, productive, and optimal? So, the next time you think about multi-tasking, do ask yourself, "what price am I willing to pay?" What are the risks I am exposing myself and others to?

Wherever a person's treasure is, there is his heart. (Jesus).

66 Legacy versus inheritance

Recently, I was at a funeral for a close family friend who was well up in years. She had moved several times from different countries and states, spending her latter years in Georgia. The pastor noted that usually, when someone dies at this age (based on his experience), there is not a large attendance as many of the people or acquaintances of the deceased would have already passed on or are unable to attend the funeral. However, after hearing all the tributes rendered to this lady from a wide variety of individuals (many of them much younger than herself), he declared that she had indeed left a legacy that was far greater than any inheritance. An inheritance, he went on to explain, was something that you leave for others, whereas a legacy was something you leave in others. This lady touched the lives of many of the persons she met, leaving in them a lasting legacy to be "played forward."

Leaving and living a legacy then entails how well we interact with each other, how we show care and understanding (empathy, sympathy), how we encourage, how we respect and respond to others, and how we motivate and mentor. Living a legacy has no age limit and has less to do with dying and more with how we invest in the lives of others and those around us. Just saying good morning and good evening, acknowledging others, giving a word of cheer, a smile, saying thank you, calling a waiter by his or her name, and recognizing others. Just taking enough time to put the mobile device down to recognize or listen to another. These are just some simple ways we can all live and leave a legacy.

What do you want to be remembered for, the things you accumulated or the lives that you positively influenced?

67 Where there is no fuel, there is no fire

In recent years, the start of the summer season seems to be accompanied by the ubiquitous news of a new round of forest wildfires, especially in the mid-west and western states. These conflagrations consume thousands of acres of vegetation and sometimes personal property, stretching the limits and resources of the states and the federal government to get them under control. But the question that must be asked is, "why are these wildfires so expansive and invasive?" Why do they continue to repeat year after year? Part of the answer lies in the fact that there seems to be a continuous supply of fuel available in the form of vegetation (trees and bushes) that feeds the fire. The fire-fighters seem to have their hands full and then have the unenviable task of sifting through the debris to determine the cause of the fire in the aftermath.

So, we fast forward to our "human forests," where we end up seeing fires in motion on a regular basis, some small, some large enough to make the news. We have these fires in homes, in families, amongst friends, in work relationships, and in other social settings. Some are pretty expansive (think Ferguson, Ukraine, Israel-Gaza), while others are small and private. The net effect of the fire is the level of damage they cause and the havoc left in their aftermath. So, how do these fires get started, and more importantly, what can we do to prevent them from spreading?

Much of these "human fires" begin as disagreements, violations of trust, unwanted invasion of personal space, abuse of property, expressions of greed, unmet expectations, unwillingness to yield, selfish desires, disrespect, and disregard for the rights/properties of others. These fires usually start out in a spate of anger, manifesting themselves through damaging/damning words that easily escalate into heated flames that consume other close associates, colleagues, friends, or family members. We retaliate with harmful words and destructive actions, sometimes resulting in physical injury which adds more fuel and fan the flames even wider and higher. We engage our friends through sympathy and empathy, getting them to support our cause that only further fuels the fire with their contributions. Before long, what is left in the wake of these "human fires" are broken relationships, lasting hurts and emotional scars, and people who no longer care for each other.

So, as you go through the forest of living, do check if you are intentionally or unintentionally starting or fueling fires. Are you adding fuel to these human conflagrations?

My freedom begins where your freedom ends- can they overlap in peace? No fuel, no fire!

68 Who has your back?

More importantly, whose back do you have? Do they know that you have their back?

69 KISS means more than keeping it simple, stupid

As we journey through life, we end up with moments where we have had to stop and think about lessons we have learned along the way. What do I need to do differently, and what adjustments, if any, do I need to make to press forward? I have discovered a simple technique that helps to get smoke out of our eyes, allowing us to hone our behavior to make greater progress in our journey and reach our goals in a more optimal manner. I called this the KISS method. And no, this does not stand for "Keep It Simple Stupid".

K: Keep doing those things that are important or valuable that are being done well.

I: Improve on those things that are important but have not been done well in the past.

S: Stop doing those things that add no value or are unimportant, things that waste time and effort.

S: Start doing those things that are important and add value to the situation that has not been done previously.

So, the next time you reach a milepost or a rest point in your journey, take the time to KISS the experience to know how to proceed.

One should use past experiences like rungs on a ladder to get to the next stage.

70 Assets versus resources

Most companies, without fail, when asked the question "what is their most important asset?" tend to respond with "our employees and or our customers." Researching the definition of an asset revealed the following: an asset is something that you own; that is, it is your property for which some value has been assigned. When an asset is deemed a property, the owner can do with it as he pleases.

We are employees of a company because we choose (acting on our own volition) to work there. Customers, too, choose to buy products or services from a company. The point is a company or business does not own its employees or customers. Technically, they are resources that companies use to realize their goals. (Notice that companies have Human Resources departments rather than Human Assets departments). Employees use their creativity and genius to generate ideas and solutions to satisfy needs/problems that people (customers) have and support business operations, while customers purchase these solutions and services to satisfy their needs or solve their problems. Employees exchange the value of their services to their employers for some form of remuneration (salaries, health benefits, paid vacation etc.). Customers, too exchange money for the service or product they receive from the company.

When a company treats its people as assets that they "own," taking them for granted rather than valuable resources that choose to work for them, they can end up mistreating them, sometimes becoming surprised when a highly valued employee decides to leave. The same goes for customers; companies who fail to recognize that they do not own their customers are more likely to go out of their way to listen to them, to care for the things they care for, and, most importantly, to show the customers that they are valued. In short, to show empathy.

So, next time you are being treated in a particular way by any organization, whether as an employee or customer, you may want to find out if you are being treated as an asset or a valued resource.

BTW - the answer to the question "What is the most valuable asset to a company?" is its data. Think about it, lose that data or compromise it, and a company could very well go out of business. Now, if you deem yourself to be "data" and you get compromised, you could go out of business.

The value of a person is not measured by his possessions but by who he is.

71 Truths and partial truths

My long commute has become more enjoyable because it affords me time to listen to audiobooks and learn new things at the same time. I recently listened to a book on the Russian Revolution (The Romanov Conspiracy) in which the author states that much of the information presented is 90% or more true. As an author, he has added some content to make for a better read. The book is full of intrigue and suspense, keeping you on the edge of your seat. The problem I am struggling with is not knowing where the truth ends and where the fiction starts as the result of a journalistic license. Some of the events and incidents described are incredible, but not being able to corroborate these with empirical evidence has left me in mental dissonance.

Therein lies our problem: when fiction is mixed in with non-fiction, lies with truth, and opinions with facts, it is very difficult to discern between the two. As human beings, we like to embellish facts, we exaggerate and stretch the truth in an attempt to convey a more convincing message or make the message less painful or more credible.

So, how about you? How do you separate fact from fiction? Do you readily mix your opinions with facts? Do you pass off your personal opinions as empirical facts? How do you really know if something is true?

Mixing the truth with lies can be very much like putting a drop of cyanide in a glass of orange juice. It is hard to tell the difference by just looking at it.

Not all facts are truth; truth is "what it is," and facts are commonly held beliefs, know the difference and pursue truth.

72 There can be no quality without u and i

The launch of the government's healthcare site some years ago, the auto industry recalls, and the recent rollout of Apple's iPhone 6 have brought quality into the limelight yet again. Most recently, we had what has been called the biggest technology failure ever, when CrowdStrike's security software on which global business relies failed. This was due to a bug in the most recent software update. The failure brought much of the world's business, including airlines, financial institutions, and retail, just to name a few, to a screeching halt. And the list goes on.

Quality seems rather nebulous and yet so ubiquitous that we often take it for granted except when the resultant loss of value from the product or service is significant or widespread. Quality is a way of life and is not confined only to commercial products but to every facet of life. Many academics and quality professionals have provided a variety of definitions of quality. For me, quality is simply this: "doing the right things right all the time in ensuring that the persons on the other end are satisfied."

We tend to assess quality by the lack of the perceived value derived from the use of services or products produced by others. We do not often think that as the supplier of those services or products, we, too, fail to deliver what is expected and hence contribute to poor quality. Here are some everyday basic examples: waking up to take a shower and there is no electricity or warm water, doing something for someone without them expressing thanks, talking to another person while they are fully engaged on their mobile device, asking for a hot cup of coffee and getting a hot cup of tea with milk, delivering the status report late with no prior warning.

Quality is the accepted norm that things will continue to work as they should; people will do what is expected of them and be considerate of others. We very often look at quality from the point of view of the recipient or user of the service or deliverable, but it bodes us well to look at quality from the perspective of being a supplier. Are we doing the right thing? Have we taken into consideration the impact on the person on the other side who will use or rely on my contribution?

At the end of the day there can be no true quality without u and i.

73 How heavy are your words?

I was at the airport some time ago when I overheard a mother berating her young child. The child had done something wrong, and the mother was not ashamed to "discipline" the child on the spot, or so she thought. She called him derogatory names, that he would amount to no good and that he was just like his father (and that was not a compliment). The child, as you can imagine, seemed devastated by his mother's attack. Quite obviously, this was not the first time.

What we sometimes fail to understand is the weight of our words on others, especially those whose lives we influence or those we have authority over. My wife reminds me, when sharing information with others, to always consider the weight and impact of the information on the hearer. Is the information age-appropriate? Can the hearers adequately handle the weight of the information being shared with them? How will it impact them? What will they do with it? We are often surprised that information shared in confidence with others somehow becomes public knowledge. Did we ever give thought to the fact that the information being shared was too much for that person to hold on to and keep by himself? In short, the information was just too "heavy"; they had to get others to share the load.

In hierarchical organizations, the weight of the words of a leader in the upper echelons of the organization tends to be more profound and impactful on those in the lower levels of the organization. Notice that we can say things to our friends, and they seem to handle it fine, but share the same information with someone who is more of an acquaintance, and you can see how two people respond differently. No one would ask a 2-year-old to carry a 50-pound bag, but do we take into consideration that we do the same thing when we share information with others who are not in a position/maturity "age" to handle the weight of the information adequately? Sometimes, we share too much information; sometimes, the information shared is too significant for a person to manage adequately. Sometimes, the information shared is too pressing and demanding.

So, next time you are sharing information with another person, do ask the question, "Can the person really handle all this information that I am sharing, or will it be overloading them?" And please let me know if this is TMI.

When you are hungry, it is not everyone you meet you should tell – (Jamaican proverb).

74 Throwing dirt

I remember, as kids growing up on a farm, what fun we had playing in the dirt. Ever so often, one of the more rambunctious and obstreperous kids would end up throwing dirt at another. This sometimes culminated in a fight or, worse yet, adult intervention where the outcome was even worse. Fast-forward to adulthood, and we discover that we still have a lot of kids running around in adult bodies. Take, for instance, political campaigns where this behavior is avidly displayed by the contenders for the office at hand. The candidates invariably resort to throwing dirt at their opponents without fail. That is where a candidate finds all the negative (true or not) information and events to plaster his opponent with, with the intent of making him look bad in the sight of the electorate. When a candidate becomes extremely desperate, it is not unusual for him not just to throw dirt but mud at his opponent. The intention is that this mud will stick and leave a lasting image in the minds of the voters.

How is it that, as supposedly a more mature and understanding society, we regularly devolve into such degenerate behavior? We end up throwing dirt on others when we intentionally embarrass them before others. We call out their negative traits, remind them of past failures, we recall their mistakes and shortcomings with the sole intention of making them look bad in their eyes and others.

One of the things we quickly discovered as kids is that when we throw dirt on others, our hands and sometimes our clothes get dirty as well. The meaner kids would use mud with the intention that this would stick and make it harder for the other person to remove it from their clothes, hair, or skin.

So, the next time you are tempted to throw dirt at someone else, do take into consideration that it will leave your hands dirty.

When we throw dirt at others, we give up ground.

75 Sticking together works

My two sons never ceased to provide us with opportunities to test our parenting skills. The younger of the two was in the habit of complaining about his brother, especially when he thought he was not being treated fairly. Invariably, he would run to us, declaring that his brother had offended him in one way or another. Well, we had to put a stop to this as we believed that our younger son was "milking" the situation for his own good, knowing that in the past, we tended to side with him. We had to stop his whining (whether justified or not) and his older brother from taking advantage of the situation. After all, they were brothers, and they should know how to live lovingly with each other (the way I did with my brother). So, I thought I would try a new tactic in disciplining to get this done.

So, the next time my younger son came in with his usual tattle (did I say he was a hypochondriac in the making), I sprung my plan into action. On this occasion, I did not seek to get to the truth; I simply called his older brother. As to be expected, he was not in the most pleasant of moods, especially towards his brother, which was simply perfect for my little plot. I listened to both sides of their stories and then pronounced that they would just have to learn to live together in harmony. So, without further ado, to help them do this, they would have to hug each other in a tight bear hug for 10 minutes, face to face at that. Well, as you can imagine, this was the longest 10 minutes in their lives. In their eyes, I was not the greatest dad at that point, but I was more interested in the long-term outcome. Well, fast forward to 15 years later into adulthood, and I am happy to say that the two brothers now live harmoniously together in a house that the older brother bought. They have become symbiotic.

Sometimes, when we are confronted with problems, it makes sense to think of other options that can provide better lasting results.

How about you? Do you look for alternate options to remediate situations that have gone awry? Do you think outside the box for solutions to make that difference, or do you default to the tried and proven methods that normally bear the same results? Think about ways you can do things differently that will provide long-term results.

Togetherness at its best is unbeatable, at its worst, unbearable.

76 Walls are a way of life

Walls, walls, they are all around, so it seems. Depending on the side of the wall you find yourself on. A wall may indeed be a good thing or a bad thing. Think about it, if there are dangers around, you would want to be on the inside of the wall where it offers some protection from that danger. However, if the wall is an impediment to free movement and access, then it is undesirable. On my recent trip to Israel and Palestine, I had a first-hand encounter with the impact of walls on people. The Israeli government is in the process of building a wall (some 430 miles long) to protect its citizens from attacks from Palestinians. The Palestinians, on the other hand, see the wall as a blockade to peace, land encroachment and restriction of their ability to freely enter Israel to work. The wall in some places is over 25 feet high. In one of the areas visited, the wall was built almost in one man's front yard. This became his new view. So, instead of having to look at this ugly grey wall, he planted an olive tree to block the site of the wall. In other areas, people had decorated the walls with murals, poetry and "inspirational" graffiti.

For many and most of us, life is just like that. Without warning, walls may spring up in our front yards and backyards. Walls that are built not by our design or our desire. Walls that are unwelcome and intrusive, walls that impede our progress, walls that stifle our growth, walls that are too tall to surmount, walls that seem impenetrable. So, the question is, what do you do with these walls that sometimes pop up in your lives? Do we curse them and those who were responsible for building them? Do we make the most of them by "painting olive trees" or decorating them? Do we punch holes in them, or do we attempt to climb over them?

So, as you look at the unwanted walls in your lives, ask yourself: what are you doing to make the most of your wall?

What I do with my wall defines how I shape my world.

77 Primary motivators

I have discovered that much of our behavior is driven by what I call the eight primary motivators. These are intrinsic drivers that determine how we act throughout life. Why primary? Because these cannot be reduced or decomposed to lower levels. So, what are these?

1. **Self-preservation:** This is our desire to survive, to stay alive, and to protect our space, possessions, and territories. Our desire to express and protect our freedom and independence. "This is mine. I own it, and I have a right to it."

2. **Pleasure:** This is self-gratification, our drive to appease our senses and provide us with good feelings (expressed through laughter, happiness, and joy).

3. **Pride**: Our sense of self-worth and esteem drives our desires for recognition from others and personal satisfaction in who we are and what we have done and accomplished. (Trophies, awards, photographs, competition, coming first).

4. **Curiosity of knowledge**: Our desire to know things, to research, to explore, to figure things out (science, schools, universities, movies, books, education).

5. **Companionship**: Our desire to be with other people, to interact and socialize freely with those we like, or we are comfortable with. (Families, friends, gangs, teams).

6. **Love and Compassion**: Our desire to help those who are in need, hurting, or less fortunate than we are. A focus on helping and giving of ourselves to others. (Hospitals, charities, philanthropy).

7. **Justice**: Our desire to see that the right things are done and knowing that the wrong or those who have done the wrong are held accountable for their actions; that evil does not win in the end. (Morality, courts, jails, prisons, laws, lawsuits, judges, revenge, getting even).

8. **Worship**: Our desire to look up to or hold some entity in high esteem that we deem more successful, powerful, or accomplished than ourselves. Larger than life figures that we pay obeisance to. (Religion, entertainers, sports heroes, business icons, role models, etc.).

I am sure you can come up with your own lists, but I tend to see many of these motivators at play continuously in our lives. Listen to terms such as "It is not fair, that's mine, I love you, I feel great, I want to know, how can I help you, how are you?" and you can see a mix of these motivators at work in the background.

The actions of a person like a ship are driven by the engine from within.

78 What box are you wearing?

Very often, in moments of empathy and as caring individuals, we tend to tell others, "I know what you are going through; I, too, have been there." The noble intent is to encourage the other person and let them know we are standing with them. Well, I was unpleasantly surprised recently when a person made those comments to someone who had a traumatic experience based on the response given: "No, you do not know what I have gone through, and neither can you relate to all of the ups and downs that life has put me through to really feel and fully know what I am going through now!" Ouch!

As we experience life, we live it through a box or framework. This box conditions our thinking and how we interpret, act, and respond to life's events. Here are what the walls of this box represent. What makes up your box?

1. **Beliefs**: These are concepts we accept, for the most part, to be true until we have justifiable reasons to change them. **One's belief does not constitute truth.**

2. **Values:** These are pivotal and deep-seated ideals we hold dear and deem to be true, and we rarely and slowly change, which makes it very hard for us to release.

3. **Culture**: Traditional behavioral norms and their influence on us by our immediate society, friends, families, and the media.

4. **Environment:** The framework of society, education, religion, family, work settings, entertainment channels, government, and their impact on our lives

5. **Experience and history**: How we have handled and responded to situations in the past, how these have affected us for better or for worse, and how we use these to make decisions in the present.

When any of the sides of our box are vastly different from others, it sometimes makes it very difficult for us to be in harmony or agreement or fully understand the other person's situation or perspective. Remember, we can never know what another person is going through until we get into their box and see life the way they do. This is more than walking in their shoes as very often their shoe size is different from ours.

Do not judge me until you have worn my boxes.

79 What type of sea are you?

Recently, I had the pleasure of visiting Israel as part of the team from my local church. One of the more interesting takeaways was visiting the Sea of Galilee, the Jordan River, and the Dead Sea. While at the Sea of Galilee, we were able to go boating and had a wonderful lunch with fish caught from the sea (which gives a new meaning to fresh fish). This was followed up with a visit to the Jordan River, where the high point was watching people of a variety of countries getting baptized. The final stop was the visit to the Dead Sea (the lowest point on earth below sea level). There, one could float in the Dead Sea.

So here we have two seas, yet both were vastly different. The Sea of Galilee was vibrant, with a gentle breeze and fishing, and actually emptied into the Jordan River. The Jordan River empties into the Dead Sea, which has no outlet. The Dead Sea had no intrinsic living organism in it. In short, it was a dumping ground, a collection point for all the minerals being transported by the river. The fact that it had over eons collected so much mineral salts has made it so dense that one can easily float on it.

This made me think that in life, we run into people who represent both types of seas and even rivers. There are those who, like the Sea of Galilee, provide life sustenance to others and provide the means for others to grow and flourish. They do not harbor things that can make them dense. Rather, they are renowned for giving. They give and forgive quickly. Those who mirror the Dead Sea are takers; they do not release to others, they hoard, they keep long memories of past hurt, they do not share, and believe it is all about them. Theirs is to hold on to everything good and bad that flows into them. Over time, they become dense and do very little to promote healthy living.

So, which of these two seas best reflect you, the Sea of Galilee (life) or the Dead Sea (death)? Do you find yourself giving of yourself to others or holding on to everything, not willing to let go or share? Which do you want to be remembered for, one who shares or one who hoards and clings on to all things?

The best in life is earned by those who give of themselves to others more so than those who only take from others.

80 Changing the future

No matter how hard we try, we cannot change our future; no more than we can change our past.

Some may readily disagree on the point that we cannot change our future. Yes, they may agree that we cannot change our past. However, they would argue that we can indeed change our future. Only the Lord knows our future; the choices we make determine our future. The decisions we make in the present no doubt influence the outcome and what happens in the future. If we had indeed known what would happen to us in the future and did not, then that would not have been our future. Our future is exactly what happens to us, just like the past.

I continue to engage with people who have made decisions and choices that have turned out to be counterproductive, sometimes even harmful. They bemoan the fact that if they had done this or that, then the situation would have turned out differently. That is wishful thinking on their part; at the end of the day, the steps and intersections we experience in life are just what they should be. I know many will disagree with this notion but take the time to carefully think about it. We cannot change our future. Every thought and action taken landed us where we were and are then and now, respectively.

When our lives have been exhausted, the path taken is the only one that was taken. Yes, looking back, we could say if we did that or that, then the outcome would have been different. So, we live our lives to the fullest, knowing that our future is the sum outcome of the choices we make today and the intersection of what life throws at us. Think about that.

Life is not what it makes of us; rather, it is what we make of it.

Life is like a bed of roses, use the thorns as rungs in a ladder to get to the petals of your dreams.

81 Lessons from a baton

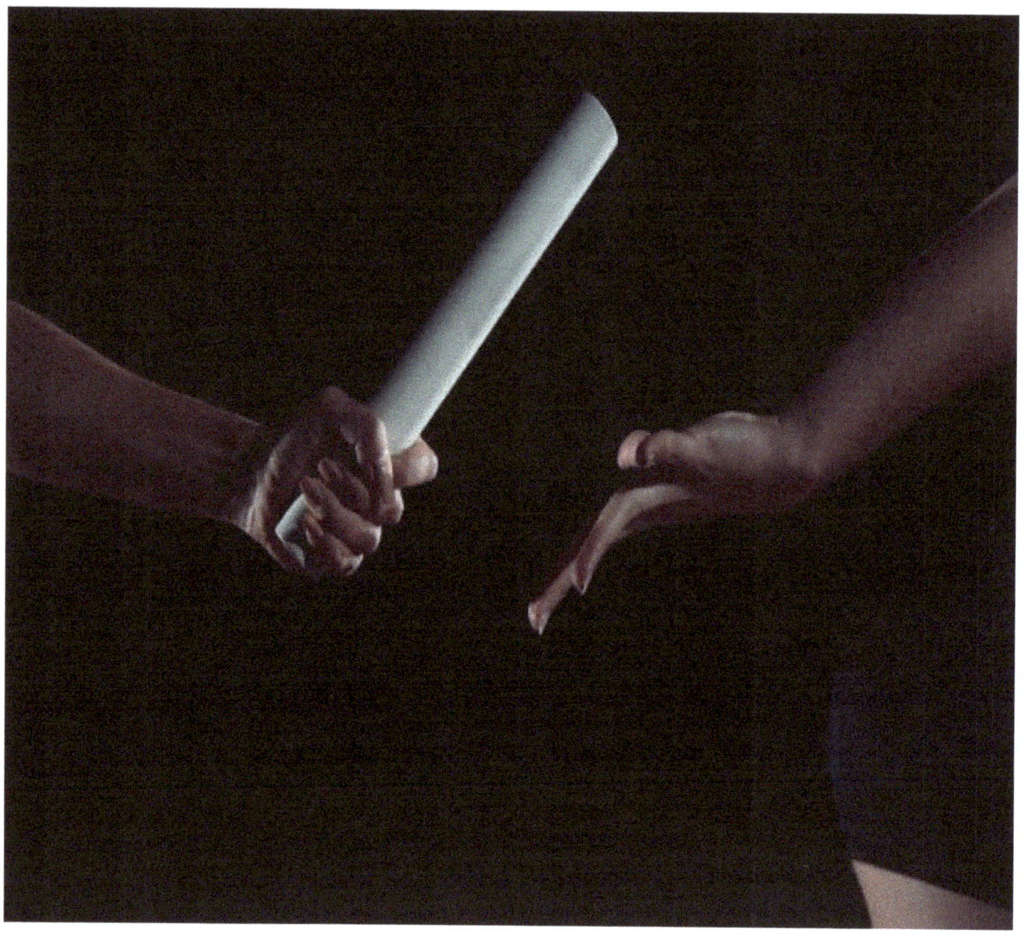

I was born in a country where sprinting is a given, more so at the world-class level. In recent times, Jamaicans have dominated the sprint events at all levels of international competition. At the time of writing, the country had the fastest male of all time and the second-fastest female of all time. Who has not heard of Usain Bolt, the speed monster? Scientists claim that based on his height (6 feet, 5 inches), his body should not perform the way it does. But he holds the world record for the fastest time ever run in the 100 meters at 9.58 seconds in the World Championships in 2019

On August 11, 2012, Bolt and his teammates created a new world record in the 4X100 relay of 36.84 seconds. So, dividing this time by 4, the average time of each athlete running their segment of the 100 meters was 9.21 seconds, 0.37 seconds faster than the individual world record.

So, what can we learn from this phenomenon? Teamwork (home or work) will always beat out individual efforts when done right. Running a relay is a team event; speed does not always guarantee a win, and you must exchange the baton in a fixed corridor. You must run in your lane; you have to exchange the baton without dropping it. At the baton exchange, the runner receiving the hand-off does not start off from a position of rest, as is the case with a 100-meter individual sprint. The runner is well in flight by the time the baton is received.

Let's look then at how we work as teams. By teams, I mean two or more persons engaged in some activity for a desired outcome. Do we know who our teammates are? Do we know what our "batons" are and who we are passing this off to? Do we run in our lanes or adopt an "anything gives" attitude? Do we efficiently hand off work to other team members, or just leave it there for them to pick it up for them to start from ground zero? Are we all running in the same direction, towards the same goal and finish line? The full impact of being part of a team and working in a team is the fact that we support each other. As a member of a team, we provide that extra lift and boost to get us to the next stage.

You cannot perform a baton exchange or shake one's hand with a closed fist.

82 Balance - it keeps us even-keeled

I have this crepe myrtle tree growing in my backyard adjacent to the house. The tree over the years, had become top-heavy, with the branches starting to brush against the house. I decided to remove those branches closest to the house, but now the tree was lop-sided and off-balance and leaning heavily to one side. Shortly thereafter, I noticed that new branches were being generated from some of the older ones on the side where I had removed the previous branches. The tree was correcting its balance right before my eyes!

We, too, have instances where life throws us off balance. We have encounters, incidents, or accidents that leave us like that tree, looking all lop-sided and off balance.

As we all like to say, life throws us curve balls. This very often is manifested in situations or circumstances that we are the least prepared for. The situation at hand puts a tax and strain on us, whether it is our own making, an accident, or something caused by others. So, how do we respond when our branches get lopped off?

What if instead of accepting the fact that we are off-balance and that is the way life is, we do what is necessary to get back into the right balance? What if we forgive the wrong instead of walking around with the hurt? What if we engage with the person who chopped off my branch rather than avoiding them? What if we take time to re-focus, re-adjust, and change our perspective to better find that balance?

So, take some time and do a balance test to see how much you are leaning toward one side or the other, and take the necessary steps to adjust.

I am most balanced when I have no decisions to make, which is a decision I have to make.

83 Knowing when to let go

It is sometimes amazing to see how we act as human beings. From time to time, we find ourselves in painful situations or, worse yet, situations that are detrimental to our well-being and health, only to ask ourselves later on, what was that for?

It is said that in certain parts of South America, the natives have an ingenious way of catching monkeys. They would normally carve out a hole in a tree, just big enough for the monkey to slip its hand through. They would then place some bait for the monkey. Invariably, the monkey would show up, placing its hand in the hole with the farmer hiding nearby. It would then grab onto the bait by clasping it and, in so doing, making a fist. The farmer would then come along and capture the monkey because, having made a fist to grasp the bait, it did not want to release the bait in order to free its hand. The monkey's fist quite obviously was too big to come through the hole, and even in the presence of impending danger, it did not want to let go of the bait.

So, there you have it. We, just like these monkeys, find ourselves grasping ever so tightly on some item that may put our well-being at risk. It could be a bad habit, a relationship, or a situation that is completely unhealthy, yet for some reason, we fail to undo the fist, to release and let go. We hold on until we invariably encounter an undesirable outcome.

Are you holding on to anything that is injurious to your health or well-being? Is your hand so tightly formed in a fist clinging on to that which could do you harm in the long run?

Take the time to evaluate the situation and predicament and know when to let go.

When the pain of holding on is greater than the pain of letting go, one will let go.

84 Weaponizing of words

In more recent times, it seems that every slight or misfortune in life is the result of some discrimination, where someone, an organization, or an institution has prevented us from fully experiencing the "rights" due to us. We tend to use this as our first form of defense when things do not go our way, especially when people are involved.

In the public domain, we see many situations where someone who believes he did not get what he should see this as discrimination. In fact, the word discrimination has become our weapon of choice and is very often used as the first line of defense when we do not get our way in a situation relative to others who do. The word discrimination has taken a bad rap for our misfortunes.

But let us think about this for a while. Discrimination is not a bad thing. We all exercise discrimination in our everyday lives at every turn. By discrimination, I mean making a choice of doing one thing over another, selecting one thing over another, sometimes at the expense of another.

Employers practice blatant discrimination when they hire or promote one individual over another who has more skills that match the job requirements. Airlines discriminate amongst their passengers as to who gets to sit in which class on the plane based on their ability to pay. When we give out awards and rewards, we are practicing discrimination by giving to some and not to all. Universities practice outright discrimination when grades are used to select some students over others for placement, advancement, or even graduation. We as individuals practice discrimination in so many areas of our lives, where we shop who we select as friends. You get my point.

Instead of using discrimination wantonly as a bad word, we should use it in conjunction with the attribute being used to make the selection or determination and the proper context. That attribute should not prevent a person from enjoying the same rights and privileges – whether it's race, gender, height, weight, age, physical condition, ethnicity, or socio-economic status where the benefits should be open and accessible to all. Why should a very obese person be asked to pay for two airline seats?

So, the next time you hear someone use the words," That's discrimination" or "You are discriminating against..." find out the context and the qualifying attribute that should be used.

A soft answer turns away wrath; a word fitly spoken is like apples of gold in pictures of silver. (The Bible)

www.ingramcontent.com/pod-product-compliance
Ingram Content Group UK Ltd.
Pitfield, Milton Keynes, MK11 3LW, UK
UKHW061954290726
14090UKWH00021B/1229